Philemon's Problem
The Daily Dilemma of the Christian

By the same Author:
Catholic Theories of Biblical Inspiration
Since 1810: A Review and Critique
(Cambridge University Press, 1969)

Philemon's Problem

Problem

The Daily Dilemma of the Christian

James Tunstead Burtchaell, C.S.C.

Life in Christ,
division of ACTA,
Foundation for Adult Catechetical Teaching Aids,
201 East Ohio
Chicago, Ill. 60611

To
My Students at Notre Dame
Who
Learned These Things With Me
and
Much Else Besides

Nihil Obstat: Charles E. Sheedy, C.S.C.
Imprimi Potest: Howard J. Kenna, C.S.C.
Imprimatur: †Leo A. Pursley, D.D.
                         Bishop of Fort Wayne-South Bend

March 6, 1973

Copyright © 1973 by ACTA Foundation, Chicago, Ill.
ISBN: 0-914070-05-3

Library of Congress # 73-88935

Manufactured in the United States of America

Contents

Introduction: Philemon's Problem   1

1. The Father of Jesus, and Strange Gods Before Him   11
2. His Father's Son, Firstborn of Many Brethren   33
3. A Disquieting Ethic   53
4. An Ethic Both Personal and Social   85
5. The Rituals of Jesus, the Anti-Ritualist   123
6. The Prodigal Father, and How His Sons Draw
    Close to Him   145

Afterword   173

Introduction:
Philemon's Problem

To Philemon:

From Paul, a prisoner of Christ Jesus and from our brother Timothy; to our dear fellow worker Philemon, our sister Apphia, our fellow soldier Archippus and the church that meets in your house; wishing you the grace and the peace of God our Father and the Lord Jesus Christ.

I always mention you in my prayers and thank God for you, because I hear of the love and the faith which you have for the Lord Jesus and for all the saints. I pray that this faith will give rise to a sense of fellowship that will show you all the good things that we are able to do for Christ. I am so delighted, and comforted, to know of your love; they tell me, brother, how you have put new heart into the saints.

Now, although in Christ I can have no diffidence about telling you to do whatever is your duty, I am appealing to your love instead, reminding you that this is Paul writing, an old man now and, what is more, still a prisoner of Christ Jesus. I am appealing to you for a child of mine, whose father I became while wearing these chains: I

1

mean Onesimus. He was of no use to you before, but he will be useful to you now, as he has been to me. I am sending him back to you, and with him—I could say—a part of my own self. I should have liked to keep him with me; he could have been a substitute for you, to help me while I am in the chains that the Good News has brought me. However, I did not want to do anything without your consent; it would have been forcing your act of kindness, which should be spontaneous. I know you have been deprived of Onesimus for a time, but it was only so that you could have him back for ever, not as a slave any more, but something much better than a slave, a dear brother; especially dear to me, but how much more to you, as a blood brother as well as a brother in the Lord. So if all that we have in common means anything to you, welcome him as you would me; but if he has wronged you in any way or owes you anything, then let me pay for it. I am writing this in my own handwriting: I, Paul, shall pay it back—I will not add any mention of your own debt to me, which is yourself. Well then, brother, I am counting on you, in the Lord; put new heart into me, in Christ. I am writing with complete confidence in your compliance, sure that you will do even more than I ask.

There is another thing: will you get a place ready for me to stay in? I am hoping through your prayers to be restored to you.

Epaphras, a prisoner with me in Christ Jesus, sends his greetings; so do my colleagues Mark, Aristarchus, Demas and Luke.

May the grace of our Lord Jesus Christ be with your spirit.

Philemon was a rather prosperous, bourgeois citizen in the town of Colossae, about 100 miles inland from the Aegean Sea in Asia Minor (now Western Turkey). He was a Christian, and he stood prominently among the little band of believers in that town, who used to meet in his home to pray and sup together. No record survives of his character, but such standing as he does enjoy in recorded history all derives from the fact that one of his household slaves, called Onesimus, one day ran away.

He made for the nearby coastal city of Ephesus, a brawling seaport where it would be easy for a fugitive to mingle anonymously among the transient population that crowded the streets. Certain elements in the underworld there were at the time rallying round a Jewish detainee, Paul, who had been a public enemy at Ephesus ever since the riots that attended his first appearance there. Enthralled by the way of life Paul was teaching, the slave became a Christian himself and was baptized into the group.

Onesimus might have expected his new comrades to provide him with still safer shelter. Paul, he knew, had a network of connections across Achaia and Macedonia and even as far away as Rome: an underground *via*, so to speak, of fellow-believers who could harbor him at a secure distance from the provincial officers who hunted down renegade slaves, and returned them in irons to face the death penalty. It must have come as a shock when Paul decided instead that he would have to return home. To afford Onesimus some protection in Colossae, Paul sent him along with Tychicus, his personal courier who was at the time delivering a letter from Paul to the Christians of that town. (In the letter Paul smoothly commends his associate courier "Onesimus, that dear and faithful brother who is a fellow citizen of yours" [4,9].)

For an irate Philemon something more was required; Paul sat down and wrote him a brief but very personal message, reproduced above. It may be the only extant document among the apostle's writings which Paul penned in his own hand.

The letter to Philemon is a masterpiece of persuasion. After the usual courteous greetings to the householder, his wife, and son, Paul notes how well spoken of Philemon was for his hospitality to fellow-Christians. This encourages Paul to ask him to take Onesimus back. There is, of course, the matter of the master's rights under law. Paul never speaks directly to this, but does enter a discreet mention of his own imprisonment. With Paul afoul of the law for preaching pub-

licly the Jesus who was being worshipped at private gather-
ings beneath Philemon's own roof, the gentleman at Colossae
was not in a position to be scrupulous over the civil statutes.

Beyond the law remained the master's rightful grievance
that his chattel and slave had cheated and abandoned him
(there is some ambiguity in the text here; it appears that
Onesimus may not have run off empty-handed). Paul deli-
cately reminds Philemon that he is himself in debt to Paul.
Philemon had not caught his faith from Epaphras, the itinerant preacher who had started the movement in Colossae; he
was a personal convert of Paul himself. Thus the apostle
enjoyed considerable credit in that house, against which some
pretty severe liabilities might appropriately be written off.

Paul says he will not impose any duty on his friend, yet
his delicate note makes it sharply clear where duty lies. He
asks Philemon to take his slave back. What he gets is a brother in the bargain, since both were fathered into the Christian family by one same Paul. Ties of faith, says Paul, can bind
even more tightly than ties of blood. And then, at the close
of his tough-but-oh-so-gentle letter, Paul includes one last
request: keep the guest room ready, for he would like to pass
by to pay them a visit—though who knew when?

What was Philemon to make of all this? How, concretely, was he to receive this man simultaneously as offending
slave and as covenant brother? It was still his right and probably his mood to seize Onesimus and have his throat cut, as
punishment for the crime and as a lesson to like-minded
slaves. One had to go to lengths to maintain discipline, as any
slaveowner knew. But there would always be Paul to face.

There were, of course, more lenient alternatives. He
could grant Onesimus pardon, and let him off with only a
punitive mutilation (loss of a hand, perhaps, or an eye, or his
ears), or possibly just a public flogging. Suppose, however,
that Tychicus let him have a preview—as was likely—of the
other scroll he had carried from Paul, with passages such as
this which would be sure to catch his eye:

> You have stripped off your old behaviour
> with your old self, and you have put on a new self
> which will progress towards true knowledge the
> more it is renewed in the image of its creator; and
> in that image there is no room for distinction be-
> tween Greek and Jew, between the circumcised or
> the uncircumcised or between barbarian and
> Scythian, slave and free man. There is only Christ:
> he is everything and he is in everything. You are
> God's chosen race, his saints; he loves you, and you
> should be clothed in sincere compassion, in kind-
> ness and humility, gentleness and patience. Bear
> with one another; forgive each other as soon as a
> quarrel begins. The Lord has forgiven you; now
> you must do the same (Colossians 3, 9-13).

With that about to be read to his comrades in his own house
the following Sunday, it would be awkward for Philemon to
sit there among them with a brother's blood on his hands. All
the more so with Onesimus sitting there too.

A third alternative would be to reinstate Onesimus as if
he had never left. Or he could even be given less onerous
work: changed, so to speak, from a "field-nigger" to a
"house-nigger". Discipline in the household would go to
pieces, naturally. But even then Philemon might have qualms,
and worry about Paul's threatened inspection tour. Would
this be the adequate welcome Paul requested for his "dear
and faithful brother"?

A final possibility would be to give Onesimus his freedom. Manumission was a Roman slaveowner's right. But Philemon was surely no fool. He realized that if he made this
brother a freedman, within the week every slave in the household would be seeking baptism—and emancipation. Then it
would start in the houses of his friends and fellow Christian
slaveowners. Where would it all stop? A man would invite
family ruin and financial annihilation just by joining the

church. In his frustration Philemon might have been tempted to kill the troublemaker outright and bury him by dead of night, just to be rid of the mess.

Now we have no clear information how seriously Philemon felt caught in a dilemma. Presumably he worked out some solution, for the letter was later shown round to friends and eventually enjoyed public circulation. Onesimus must at least have survived. But most likely Philemon never perceived the dilemma in its starkest terms: you cannot have a brother who is your slave; you cannot have a slave who is your brother. For nineteen centuries Christians would adopt various formulae of compromise, failing a clear vision of the contradiction.

Paul himself did not pursue his own insights to their conclusions. In one of his earliest extant letters he had already instructed the Galatians that "there are no more distinctions between Jew and Greek, slave and free, male and female, but all of you are one in Christ Jesus" (3, 28; see also Romans 10, 12, and 1 Corinthians 12, 13). Yet of these three contemporary inequalities—racial, social, and sexual—Paul really tried to eradicate only the first. He started and prosecuted a virtual one-man crusade against racial discrimination that kept Jewish and Gentile Christians from ever breaking bread together. He sped to Jerusalem (a city he ordinarily avoided) in a fury when a whispering campaign developed there about his supposed softness on the integration issue. He wrote violent lines on the matter to the communities under his authority, and called Peter himself a hypocrite to his face for being a tokenist. For more than 30 years Paul made good on his word that racial prejudice, separation and disdain had no place among Christians.

Yet when it came to slaves or to wives, his words seem more like slogans than injunctions. There should be, he urges, a new quality of tenderness. But basically the traditional inequalities should remain. Slaves and wives, he told them, were to be all the more obsequious to their masters, as though they were enslaved to the Lord himself. Having thus enjoined those in inferior positions to identify their masters with Christ, Paul might then have suggested a reciprocity, identifying those in subjection also with Christ. After all, some years earlier he had written to Philippi that Jesus had assumed the condition of a slave (2, 7). Yet he cannot do it. Instead, he urges husbands and masters to be fair and compassionate because they have a common Master to face in judgment.

So strong and inexorable were these two forms of inequality and exploitation that Paul, who had over three decades of scars from his singleminded struggle for racial equity, did not see that faith in the Father of Jesus could have no peace with them. This says less to Paul's discredit than it does of mankind's obscured and prejudicial vision in every age. I have already noted that Christian leaders began to grow effectively restless about slavery only in the last century. The campaign for equal dignity, education, and opportunity for women owes much to Christian conscience, but it has been a long time coming. What are the injustices of our own time, the familar misuses of man by man which to later eyes will seem so strikingly sordid, so obviously unfair?

What of us, who resemble Philemon more than we do Paul? Philemon's problem is our problem, the problem of any believer. He was asked on his faith in Jesus to receive back into his house, to cherish as a brother (indeed to cherish as he would cherish Paul himself) a man who in their mutually accepted society was debased below all comradeship and brotherhood. Paul had bidden him take a slave as a brother. Yet Paul, himself continuing to accept slavery, failed to see the full reach of his own request. To serve Jesus' Father, to heed Paul, to embrother Onesimus, Philemon would have had to fly in the face of the society, the polity, and the economy, disenthrall his slaves one and all, and stir up a social upheaval ruinous enough that all men might become brothers.

All societies rest upon inequities—some concealed, others noticed—that make brotherhood impossible. Every age and locale has its particular and familiar slaveries. What heightens injustice is that all believers—exploiters or exploited—are equally nearsighted about the oppressions we have unwittingly learned to live with. No one cries out: the strong because they need not, the weak for they dare not. Or perhaps this is unfair: it might seem that slaves would sense injustice that owners ignore. But even slaves must have their eyes and their feelings dulled; you cannot long entertain hope for what is unattainable. So, rather than live in perpetual frustration, the enslaved man generally will not allow his conscience to become too sensitive.

Yet we are bidden take all men as brothers; and the sight of Christ crucified, all mangled yet magnificent, should warn us what the cost must be. Christians are tempted to receive his commands as so many slogans, ever trying to live at peace in societies where men cannot effectually be brothers as they are told to be. Whereas social, political, and economic revolution are continually indicated by Christian faith, we prefer to come to terms with what we have grown to regard as familiar and congenial. Christ's baptism of fire is quenched so disappointingly by our own rites of water. Christians do not refuse brotherhood; but they often fail to see what it requires, because they cannot bear to see it.

Philemon's problem goes even deeper. It is not only that he fails to receive clear, concrete imperatives from his church; nor that his vision of what Christ requires is perforce obscured by his own vested interests and the blurred perspective of his own time and home; nor that massive, sacrificial generosity would be required for him to turn his life inside out on behalf of his brother, his neighbor, his enemy; nor even that he may lack the clout needed to foment a social reform in the world order that lies beyond his own household. It is the very social order that inhibits Philemon from loving Onesimus as Christ has loved him. Yet there is no social order, no revision of the economy, no advance in politics, no possible world situation that adequately conforms to the gospel or even makes room for its full realization, no revolution that does not eventually redistribute injustice. And it must then always be in a world that is flawed with blindness and greed and inequity and well-intentioned crime that Philemon lives. The Kingdom of God is near at hand, yet never quite comes; his will must be done, yet it never really is.

Sympathize with Philemon! Sympathize with any believer in Jesus Christ, for whom the impossible becomes mandatory, eternal life ruinous, brotherhood fatal. Like Philemon, we do not have the challenge put squarely to us in so many words. It grows out of a gospel that taunts us to make slaves and masters into brothers, yet is only a provocation, not an empowerment. There is no social order a Christian should not overthrow. But there is no living without a social order, and no social order is ever going to embody successfully the imperatives of Christ. We find ourselves wringing our hands in frustration at being unprofitable servants.

So we must go forward, yet without illusions. Hoping to catch fresh provocation from the origins of our belief, this book will begin with the New Testament and draw from it implications that seem simple yet are hard to see. It is a touchy task. The New Testament was written by men time-bound and myopic like ourselves, men who could not quite stretch their minds to the full measure of the mystery. Their message is ambiguous, and often at odds with itself. Their lifestyle is something less than best though perhaps missing the mark less than ours.

The theologian's dangerous venture is to catch the glow of Christ's fiery face reflected in the eyes of Matthew, Mark, and those others. This is one attempt to accept the New Testament's urging to go beyond itself. Faulty as it may be, that Testament is a classic collection of messages to which every church is answerable, and before which all of us must squirm somewhat in embarrassment. One's study and experience cannot but display to us that in our midst there abide superstition, weasel-wording cowardice, and persistent exploitation. So it ever was. This book proposes not to ignore the unhappy sight, but more emphatically to share a vision of better things put before us. I cannot decide whether it is a comfort or a disappointment to launch an undertaking with the knowledge beforehand that it does not allow of satisfaction.

1 The Father of Jesus, and Strange Gods Before Him

Voltaire once wrote in his notebook: "God made man in his image and likeness, and man has paid him back."[1] Like Caiaphas before him, the cynical French deist occasionally enjoyed the gift of making religious observations that were wiser than he knew. For a character study of deities in the mythologies and theologies of various religions discloses enough pettiness and outrage to confirm Voltaire's suspicion that most gods are patterned after their own worshippers.

The gods of the Greeks, later adopted by the Romans, were a promiscuous lot. The mythologies of both peoples

[1] *Voltaire's Notebooks*, ed. Theodore Besterman (University of Toronto Press: 1952), I, 231. This was a theme often treated by Voltaire. See the following passages of interest in his *Oeuvres Complètes* (Paris: Garnier Frères, 1880): *Homélies Prononcées à Londres en 1765*, "Deuxième Homélie sur la superstition," XXVI, 330; *Un Chrétien contre six juifs* (1776), XXIX 545-46; *La Bible enfin Expliquée* (1776), XXX, 4-5. See also *Voltaire's Correspondence*, ed. Besterman (Les Délices, Geneve: Institut et Musée Voltaire, 1961), LXVII, 106-107, No. 13588. I am grateful to Dr. Thomas Schlereth for locating these passages for me.

display the kind of family quarreling, incest, and fratricide which explain how it was that the gods managed to slip unnoticed into the battles of the men and the beds of the ladies of Athens and Rome and other similarly devout cities. As Clifford Howell once said of Olympus, "Concerning their goings-on up there the less said the better!"[2] The massive massacres of war prisoners necessary to satiate Huitzilopochtli and his annual roster of 365 associate divinities suggest that the Aztec gods were blood-thirsty as the Aztec people. Christianity records similar degradations. Saints may not be gods, but they are expected to be like God. What would God be like for the devotees of St. Florian, patron and protector against fires, whose German wayside shrines often bear the invocation: "Holy St. Florian: Save our house; let someone else's burn down"? In a similar vein, the blessing of a flag in the old Roman Ritual virtually called on God to curse the nations's enemies.

There seems, in fact, to be a repeated alignment of gods with the purposes of homicide. In his autobiography, Benvenuto Cellini tells of the time when he was besieged with Pope Clement VII within Castel San Angelo by Charles V's troops during the sack of Rome. Boastful of his marksmanship, Cellini let fly with a small artillery piece and blew in half a Spanish officer standing far off in the trenches.

> The Pope, who was expecting nothing of this kind, derived great pleasure and amazement from the sight, both because it seemed to him impossible that one should aim and hit the mark at such a distance, and also because the man was cut in two, and he could not comprehend how this should happen. He sent for me, and asked about it. I explained all the devices I had used in firing; but told

---

[2] *Of Sacraments and Sacrifice* (Collegeville, Minnesota: Liturgical Press, 1952), p. 96.

him that why the man was cut in halves, neither he
nor I could know. Upon my bended knees I then
besought him to give me the pardon of his blessing
for that homicide; and for all others I had
committed in the castle in the service of the
Church. Thereat the Pope, raising his hand, and
making a large open sign of the cross on my face,
told me that he blessed me, and that he gave me
pardon for all murders I had ever perpetrated, or
should ever perpetrate, in the service of the Apos-
tolic Church.[3]

An interesting contrast with Cellini is General George
Patton, whose memoirs betray somewhat more uneasiness a-
bout the divine pleasure:

> The first Sunday I spent in Normandy was
> quite impressive. I went to a Catholic Field Mass
> where all of us were armed. As we knelt in the mud
> in the slight drizzle, we could distinctly hear the
> roar of the guns, and the whole sky was filled with
> airplanes on their missions of destruction. . .quite
> at variance with the teachings of the religion we
> were practicing. . .
> An arresting sight were the crucifixes at road
> intersections; these were used by Signal personnel
> as supplementary telephone posts. While the
> crosses were in no way injured, I could not help
> thinking of the incongruity of the lethal messages
> passing over the wires. . .
> Christmas dawned clear and cold; lovely
> weather for killing Germans, although the thought

---

[3]*The Life of Benvenuto Cellini*, trans. and ed. John Addington Symonds
(New York: The Heritage Press [n.d.]) p. 47.

seemed somewhat at variance with the spirit of the day.[4]

Nevertheless, when the winter rains of 1944 immobilized his armored equipment, Patton impatiently directed all chaplains to pray for dry weather. Shortly before Christmas he summoned Father O'Neill, Third Army Chaplain:

> *General Patton:* "Chaplain, I want you to publish a prayer for good weather. I'm tired of these soldiers having to fight mud and floods as well as Germans. See if we can't get God to work on our side."
> *Chaplain O'Neill:* "Sir, it's going to take a pretty thick rug for that kind of praying."
> *General Patton:* "I don't care if it takes the flying carpet. I want the praying done."
> *Chaplain O'Neill:* "Yes, sir. May I say, General, that it isn't a customary thing among men of my profession to pray for clear weather to kill fellow men."
> *General Patton:* "Chaplain, are you teaching me theology or are you the Chaplain of the Third Army? I want a prayer."
> *Chaplain O'Neill:* "Yes, sir."

The prayer, printed by Army Engineers and distributed on cards with Patton's Christmas greetings on the reverse side:

> Almighty and most merciful Father, we humbly beseech Thee, of Thy great goodness, to restrain these immoderate rains with which we have had to contend. Grant us fair weather for Battle. Graciously hearken to us as soldiers who call upon

[4]George S. Patton, Jr., *War As I Knew It* (Boston: Houghton, Mifflin, 1949), pp. 95, 96, 202.

Thee that, armed with Thy power, we may advance from victory to victory, and crush the oppression and wickedness of our enemies, and establish Thy justice among men and nations. Amen.[5]

God, it appears, responded promptly with the Battle of the Bulge.

Gods are so like ourselves as to be often unsavory. This is well implied in Thomas Hardy's *Return of the Native,* when he comments on the heroine:

Eustacia Vye was the raw material of a divinity. On Olympus she would have done well with a little preparation. She had the passions and instincts which make a model goddess, that is, those which make not quite a model woman. Had it been possible for the earth and mankind to be entirely in her grasp for awhile, had she handled the distaff, the spindle, and the shears at her own free will, few in the world would have noticed the change of government. There would have been the same inequality of lot, the same generosity before justice, the same perpetual dilemmas, the same captious alteration of caresses and blows that we endure now.[6]

Christians have long thought that their God did not share in the primitive crudities of pagan deities, but there is no little evidence to deprive us of this comfort. Indeed, much of the distortion that does enter into our notion of God is introduced in each person's own primitive period: his youth. The infant development of the individual is suggestive of the evolutionary growth of mankind. It is curious to note the regressive character of the gods of our own youth. From his

[5]*Ibid.,* pp. 184-5

[6](New York: Harper and Bros., 1905), p. 77.

parents a child learns of a god who strongly disapproves of disobedience, and hitting one's brothers and sisters, and telling lies. The youngster goes to school, and finds that God also shares the many concerns—sometimes fussy ones—of his teachers. At church, the god of the parish priests has a somewhat different set of priorities: emphasis is laid upon Mass and Confession and Communion, and though it is beyond his own horizon of interest the child is aware that God also makes emphatic and recurring fiscal demands upon the parishioners. When he reaches the age for high school he finds that God's own interests have expanded: he is obsessed with sex and drinking and drugs. After he emerges from his years of youth altogether, he discovers—sometimes with resentment—that God had been used as a sanction for all those who were responsible for his discipline. When he used to cavort a bit maliciously at home, his mother might reach the end of her patience and persuasiveness and threaten, "When Daddy comes home, he'll take care of you." But if mommy and daddy are both at their wits' end, then there is always the eternal spanking to which they can and do allude. God is thus unwittingly associated with fear.

There has admittedly been a continuous tradition of alliance between religion and those who dominate. Karl Marx insisted that religion served the bourgeoisie as a tranquilizer for the exploited working classes. Peter Berger more recently has observed that the basically conservative interests of church and state have made them congenial allies throughout history.

> It is thus possible to say that Churches, understood as monopolistic combinations of full-time experts in a religious definition of reality, are inherently conservative once they have succeeded in establishing their monopoly in a given society. Conversely, ruling groups with a stake in the maintenance of the political status quo are inherently churchly in

their religious orientation and, by the same token, suspicious of all innovations in the religious tradition.[7]

Those who feel that America has freed itself of all this may meditate upon Billy Graham's presence as our own Rasputin, and conclude that the First Amendment to the Constitution is scarcely sufficient of itself to reverse a trend of centuries.

Yet one need not endorse any radical theories in political science or sociology to accept that gods have repeatedly been associated with power figures of home and city and nation, and that the deities have not always benefited from keeping such company.

Divinity seems to incur three occupational hazards, First: gods are strange. Not simply in the Isaian sense that God's thoughts are not ours, nor his ways our ways, but more by way of caprice. You can never be secure in anticipating what a god will do, how he will react. Part of the fear one has of gods is that there is no one to whom they must account for their moods—hence they tend to indulge themselves and to be arbitrary. Since the ancient and savage days when the divine hand was discerned in flood and earthquake, stillbirth and forest fire, man has been bewildered by the patterns of wrath and benevolence of the almighty. This evokes the second trait of divinity: gods are powerful. This makes the caprice of the deities all the more worrisome: in their hands they hold the keys of life and death, prosperity and destitution, war and peace. Oddly enough, gods are usually not acknowledged to have sway over the human heart, but can bear down upon man from the outside with all that fortune or misfortune represent. Lastly, gods concern themselves with what men do. It is not that they care for men so much,

[7]Peter L. Berger and Thomas Luckmann, *The Social Construction of Reality: A Treatise in the Sociology of Knowledge*, (New York: Doubleday, 1966) p. 113.

or that they necessarily make moral or ethical demands, but they do scrutinize human behavior and treat men accordingly.

It is this combination of qualities, of an unknown, a mighty, and a judgmental god, that makes most divinities distinctly unpleasant. Most gods are not quite as appealing as your better friends. Far from hankering after an eternity of their companionship, most people would probably not be anxious even to spend a weekend with their particular god or anyone else's. By a strange reversal of spookery, heaven has become haunted with the ghosts of men: men who are persistently as impersonal and as fearsome as those who domineer over their fellows. If, as Lord Acton said, power tends to corrupt, and absolute power corrupts absolutely, to whom would the aphorism be more applicable than to god? In assimilating our deities to our familiar and exploitative rulers, we have created a heaven that is peopled by the least appealing ghosts possible. We have corrupted god, and no wonder that men and their children fear him, for he can be peremptory, punitive, and petty as are we in our worst moments.

Jesus' Father: A Stranger Among Gods

Yet there has been, in Judaism and Christianity, a strange and inexorable resistance to this corruption of god. This theological tradition has been continually obscured, infected by the malignancies which, as we have argued, prey upon every religion, to the point where Jews and Christians have often (would "most often" be too blunt?) worshipped a god scarcely different from those of their pagan neighbors. Nor can we claim any method different from the common one: extrapolating from our knowledge of man, illuminated, as we believe, by inspired insight, in the hope of reaching and clarifying a concept of who lies beyond. No man has seen God; we have only ourselves as paradigms. But what Christians rejoice in is a better knowledge of a better god, since we have a new image and likeness: Jesus of Nazareth.

Those who believe that Jesus is the Son of God are not so much making a statement about Jesus as they are confessing that *he* is the one who embodies God. Like Father, like Son. Jesus, who dies for those who murder him, is the best and the ultimate model we have of what God is like. Jesus' life, death, and appearances after death are only a hint, and even an unsatisfying hint of God. God, after all, cannot be adequately revealed in human affairs, nor fittingly incarnated. All that we have, even in Jesus, is a suggestion, an allusion to what eye has not seen nor ear heard, precisely because it is too awesome to enter into the heart of man.

Nevertheless, the Father that Jesus reveals is the antithesis of our other gods. For one thing, he is not strange. He is indeed a mystery: not in the sense that he is unintelligible, that he throws us into confusion, that he is wrapped in darkness, but that on the contrary there is so much to understand, such a depth of light is exposed to us, that we can never get to the bottom of it. In this sense he is a mystery, that he is unfathomable yet invites us to know him ever more. And what is most strikingly knowable and welcome to know is that he has no moods or caprice, no arbitrary seasons of change. He has a single relentless stance towards us: he loves us. Nor is the Father of Jesus revealed to us as possessed of force. Jesus, who shuns all political influence, and refuses to call even his own followers to his aid, let alone legions of angels, is helpless before the power of any man who does him violence. Yet it is by his very bruises that we are healed. He emerges, unlike even our strange gods, as capable of touching the heart of man. He is not the god of storms or of war, but the Son of him who can leave us our freedom yet display his power in us. It is the greatest power, transforming from within. Lastly, the Father of Jesus does not scrutinize our lives. He does not judge us, for he loves even those who are evil. In a word: the Father of Jesus loves sinners. He is the only God man ever heard of who loves sinners. Gods despise sinners, but the Father of Jesus loves all, no matter what they do. But, of course, this is almost too incredible for us to accept.

The Father's love embodied in Jesus is characteristically different from our natural human way of loving. As a man, I am drawn to love various things and persons. I love the Oregon coast at sunset, Brandenburg concertos, asparagus, and my eighth grade teacher. No matter how one cares to name these reactions—savouring, loving, liking, desiring, appreciating—there is a common dynamic in them all. I am attracted by certain qualities in these other persons and things, qualities which willy-nilly I find congenial and appealing. I did not decide to like asparagus; indeed, there were early years when asparagus was not appealing (likewise, perhaps, for the eighth grade teacher). But somehow since childhood my apprehensions and evaluations changed—not by choice— and here I am liking asparagus (and Sister Kathleen Clare, wherever she may be). When I love as a man, I am drawn inexorably by the good perceived in the other. I love someone for what I find in him or her. The contrary is also true. There are some people who repel us, and we cannot decide to have it otherwise. We can be civil, we can be kind or loyal, we can marry them, but we still cannot like or love them. Behavior is a matter of choice, and it can be commanded. Human likes are autonomous reactions and often run athwart our choices.

It is obviously possible for men to relate in a more disinterested way, to move beyond their native, self-centered concern into a care for others that transcends likes and preferences. Unfortunately, by calling this movement "love" also, we obscure how radically different an act it is from that other kind of response I have been trying to describe. It requires a self-expenditure that is possible, Christians believe, only by God's enablement. It can best be seen as embodied in Jesus, who in turn suggests that kind of Father he has, that Father to whom John simply gives the name "Love."

Unlike ourselves, the Father loves men, not for what he finds in them, but for what lies within himself. It is not because men are good that he loves them, nor only good men that he loves. It is because he is so unutterably good that he loves all men, good and evil. He loves sinners. He loves the loveless, the unloving, the (for unaided us) unlovable. He does not detect what is congenial. appealing, attractive, and respond to it with his favor. Indeed, he does not respond at all. The Father is a source. He does not react; he initiates love. His is motiveless love, radiating forth eternally. And because it is creative, it originates good rather than rewarding it. Augustine had this divine priority in mind in his aphorism: *Quia amasti me, fecisti me amabilem:* In loving me, you made me lovable.

Jesus, who lives for those whose love is dead, and dies that his killers might live, reveals a Father who has no wrath. The Father cannot be offended, nor can he be pleased by what men do. This is the very opposite of indifference. The Lord who searches the heart and reins of man, who hears our most casual word, who has an eye cocked upon the sparrow, does not cherish us as we deserve—were it so we would be desolate—but as he must, unable to do otherwise. He is Love. Hard as it is for us to believe, for we neither give nor receive love among ourselves in this way, we yet believe, provoked by the life, death, and glorious appearances of the Carpenter-Messiah, that his Father is more loving, more forgiving, more cherishing than Abraham, Isaac, or Jacob would have dreamt.

What this says simply is that the Father of Jesus is gracious: his love is gratuitous. In one sense a man loves gratuitously if he is favorable to another person without his deserving it. It is a deeper and more poignant grace to be favorable to one who denies you his favor, and is hostile and injurious. The supreme grace is to be favorable in complete priority to another person's behavior. Jesus conveys that there is no motivation in God, no *quid pro quo*, there is nothing that he stands to gain. His love is utterly gratuitous in a way, as I

have said, that defies our imagination. As a response to grace
there is a corresponding spectrum of gratitude, which becomes supremely necessary when evoked by this supreme
grace: necessary, not for God's sake, but for man's. For most
gods it is a misfortune if they fail to receive their due worship
from the men they have favored, but for the Father of Jesus
there can be no misfortune. Our gratitude fills no need of his,
though it does fulfill a need in ourselves. God, then, is gracious in a way that can only be hinted at within human
events, and it is this incredible grace of his that most particularly sets him apart from all strange gods whom men have
entertained before him.

Most gods, patterned as they have been after human
lords, have been more formidable than benevolent. While
gods have at critical moments proven useful and have been
invoked with regularity, they are not persons you would care
to have around in your more casual moments. Gods, like
powerful patrons, are to be consulted in time of need, but
not supped with overly often. Most religions present man
with the prospect of joining the gods after death. The
prospect is far from appealing, if truth were told. I would
argue that if the Father of Jesus has often evoked a similar
and characteristic dread and diffidence, it is precisely because
he has been unwittingly likened by our traditions to those
pagan gods whom alone he is not prepared to tolerate.

The Gracious God in Scripture

This vision of God might best be illuminated at this point by
reference to the earliest and classic Judeo-Christian documents. But before turning to Scripture, I should clarify one
or two hermeneutical principles which I shall be using. First
of all, the Bible is a collection of literature that reflects more
than ten centuries of religious tradition. It was an argumentative millenium; and the controversies, revisions, and reversals
of thought that marked the ideological development during

this classical period are represented in and recoverable from
the books that resulted. A book written in the third century
B.C. for example, when compared to a document dating back
to the tenth century, will be found to repudiate some of the
views in the more ancient document, while refining others.
And even single books, that have been rewritten by numerous
hands over as much as 700 years, will display a diversity of
theology that has not entirely been obliterated by constant
updating. Thus, the Bible is not systematically homogeneous,
and presents its interpreter with a scatter of different beliefs
and views that are often at odds with one another. It is not
the task of the biblical reader simply to tease out the best
and most enlightened ideology available in the Bible, since
the process of development which has left a millenial residue
in Scripture has continued unabated. In a sense everything in
the Bible is obsolete for every subsequent believer. Yet as the
tradition unfolds from within itself, as earlier belief is con-
tinuously telescoping forward into later belief, the interpreter
must try to plot the trajectory of faith in its growth and
unfolding.

This is itself a creative act. There is no system of absolute norms by which one can examine and evaluate Scripture,
since the ancient traditions can be studied only from the
vantage point of the interpreter. This is why I insist it is a
creative as well as critical task. The modern critic must be
continually making choices about what is primitive and what
advanced, what regressive and what revolutionary within the
various books. His own viewpoint is fixed in a certain time
and culture. Thus his angle of retrospect is like none other,
and his interpretation must perforce be affected by it. It is
nothing that he can avoid, nor is it something he should es-
chew. But when he evaluates the texts that lie before him, he
cannot simply claim to be repeating what Jeremiah or Paul or
Luke meant. He is offering a synthesis for which he himself,
standing where he does, must claim responsibility.

The responsibility of interpretation is open to grotesque

abuse. Thus, for example, Bruce Barton in 1925 published his book, *The Man Nobody Knows,* which made out that Jesus was the original advertising executive, the harbinger of our consumer-oriented society. Pier Paolo Pasolini's film, *The Gospel According to St. Matthew,* produced in the cutting room a Jesus who is an exact replica of an Italian communist cell leader. In 1952 the *Olive Pell Bible* appeared, wherein Mrs. Pell had systematically excised all mention of sex, violence, and meat-eating, much as Martin Luther was once of a mind to omit the Epistle of James from the New Testament, since it conflicted with his theory of faith and works. These are but a few of the more violent hands that have been laid on the Bible by interpreters who were anxious for it to say but one thing, and for that one thing to be in agreement with what they believed. Yet despite these and so many other examples, there is no utterly objective standpoint available. The Bible does not agree with itself. If anyone would have a hermeneutical advantage in approaching it, it would be the believer who stands most correctly—through faith, prayer, and openness to the corrective of debate, I would believe— within the ongoing trajectory of belief as it passes through our own time.

Thus I shall in no way maintain that the particular theology of grace which this book proposes is found unchallenged within the biblical documents. There are many views of grace there. In arguing that this is the view that thrusts forward out of a common heritage within paganism, that it is the emergent and peculiar contribution of Judeo-Christianity, I must take responsibility for the hindsight I possess, and realize that it depends not simply on a scientific handling of the literature, but on the worth of my own stance today. It is a view that claims to be inspired by the Bible, but many other views, some quite adverse, have boasted similar inspiration. My remarks on Scripture will not be very extensive, and will be more by way of illustration than of proof, since the view of grace that is offered has not so much been explicitly denied by Christians as it has been inadvertently neglected, or felt to be too incredible to accept. But no presentation, no matter how systematic and minute, could hope to offer proof.

The literature of Israel broods repeatedly over the problem of its relation to Yahweh. On the one hand, his choice of the sons of Abraham, Isaac, and Jacob is gratuitous, and since he is in sovereign control of the affairs of men, he is mighty enough and more so to ensure the faithfulness of his people. On the other hand, there is the constant worry that, no matter how gracious their Lord, the Hebrews could always anger him beyond recall. The tension is embodied in two different covenant arrangements. The covenant made between the Lord and David is strong on grace: God unilaterally chooses David, the inauspicious shepherd boy, to be king, and promises him that his descendants will rule over Israel forever. God will adopt David's son as his very own. Should he stray into infidelity, never fear: the Lord would find brief disasters sobering enough to bring him back to his senses. The theology of this covenant of guaranteed grace is most clearly expressed in 2 Samuel 7. The covenant with Abraham is patterned after that with David: God intervenes on his own initiative, makes promises that have no conditions attached, and guarantees that his purpose is not to be thwarted (Genesis 12ff).

The covenant with Moses at Sinai, by contrast, is quite bilateral. The Lord is still the initiator: the rescue from Egypt was by his design and his repeated intervention. But his choice of the sons of Israel requires that they bind themselves to follow his Law, and understand well that should they fail in the undertaking then he will most assuredly have to abandon them. Besides the long passages in Exodus which describe this covenant, it may perhaps best be seen in Deuteronomy 28, where Moses quite cleanly puts to the people the two alternatives: obedience and life, or neglect of the Law and death.

Neither of the two models ever quite overcame the other. The Davidic covenant was naturally favored by the

monarchy, and the Mosaic covenant inspired the critics of the
king, the prophets. Most often they are not seen as clearly
antithetical, as in the following passage from Deuteronomy:

> If Yahweh set his heart on you and chose
> you, it was not because you outnumbered other
> peoples: you were the least of all peoples. It was
> for love of you and to keep the oath he swore to
> your fathers that Yahweh brought you out with his
> mighty hand and redeemed you from the house of
> slavery, from the power of Pharaoh king of Egypt.
> Know then that Yahweh your God is God indeed,
> the faithful God who is true to his covenant and
> his graciousness for a thousand generations towards
> those who love him and keep his commandments,
> but who punishes in their own persons those that
> hate him. He is not slow to destroy the man who
> hates him; he makes him work out his punishment
> in person. You are therefore to keep and observe
> the commandments and statutes and ordinances
> that I lay down for you today (7, 7-11).

There seem to be two Gods here. On the one hand,
there is a Lord who chooses Israel irrespective of Israel's
merits. Yet there is also the Lord who will continue to cherish Israel only on the ground of her merits. The Old Testament oscillates between the two ideologies, trying to sidestep
the hazards of each. If you have a God who is totally gratuitous, then what possible serious motive could you have for
being righteous? But if being at peace with God depends
upon your being righteous, how can you call his blessing a
gift?

One theme which strove to weave the two theologies
together was that of continual forgiveness and reconversion.
In the book of Judges a repeated cycle is set up: apostasy,
punishment, conversion, and deliverance. Over the course of
a dozen generations, each time the people forgot Yahweh and

his Law, he unleashed one of the hostile, neighboring tribes upon them. They repented, and he at first withstood them in his anger. But they always wore him down eventually. " 'You on your part have turned from me and served other gods; and so I shall rescue you no more. Go and cry to the gods you have chosen. Let them rescue you in your time of trouble.' The Israelites answered Yahweh, 'We have sinned. Do with us as you think fit; only do rescue us today.' They got rid of the foreign gods that they had, and served Yahweh, and he could bear Israel's suffering no longer" (Judges 10, 13-16). At the moment when Judah was destroyed by Babylon and taken into exile, Jermiah thought briefly that there was an end to this cycle of apostasy and forgiveness: the sons of Israel were to be repudiated forever. But his fellow-prophets in Babylon quickly insist that there is no end to the softheartedness of their God. In his long and most poignant oracle, comparing the history of the people to a long marriage wherein a for-giving husband is ever reclaiming his adulterous bride, Ezekiel concludes with the Lord's final words: " 'I am going to renew my covenant with you; and you will learn that I am Yahweh, and so remember and be covered with shame, and in your confusion be reduced to silence, when I have pardoned you for all that you have done' " (16, 62-63). Just a few years later his colleague in exile, Deutero-Isaiah wrote similarly:

> Shout for joy, you heavens; exult, you earth!
> You mountains, break into happy cries!
> For Yahweh consoles his people
> and takes pity on those who are afflicted.
> For Zion was saying, "Yahweh has abandoned me,
> and Lord has forgotten me".
> Does a woman forget her baby at the breast,
> or fail to cherish the son of her womb?
> Yet even if these forget,
> I will never forget you. (Isaiah 49, 13-15)
>
> I did forsake you for a brief moment,

but with great love will I take you back.
In excess of anger, for a moment
I hid my face from you.
But with everlasting love I have taken pity on you,
says Yahweh, your redeemer. (Isaiah 54, 7-8)

Still, this very theme of compassion brings with it the
suspicion that Yahweh could not really get on without Israel,
that his raison d'être as a God was irrevocably tied up with
this people. How could you take the anger of such a god
seriously? Indeed, how gracious would he really be, if he had
no choice but to cherish Israel? There is a constant paradox:
God could at any time reject Israel; yet he was not the sort of
God who rejected his own.

The paradox flows over into the New Testament. There
one is commonly reminded that only those who do the will
of Jesus' Father in heaven will enter the kingdom (Matthew
7,21). Those who indulge in fornication, idolatry and sor-
cery, drunkenness, etc. will certainly not inherit the kingdom
(Galatians 5, 19-21). Jesus' closest neighbors who fail to take
him seriously and to repent will be cast down to hell (Matthew 11, 20-24; Luke 10, 13-15). Yet, it is never the will of
the Father in heaven that any of his weak ones be lost (Matthew 18, 12-14; Luke 15, 3-7); he will leave the 99 in order
to seek the single stray. The entire purpose of Jesus' mission
is to reconcile men to his Father, and it is precisely this
notion of *purpose* that suggests a unity from within the paradox.

The inner core of the gospel is the story of Jesus' death
and resurrection. The gospel assigns responsibility for this
tragedy-turned-triumph to various persons: to Judas, to the
other disciples, to the Romans, to the Jews, to Jesus himself,
and to his Father. The disciples, of course, are not even present at Jesus' death and are bewildered by the resurrection;

most likely they are out of town, fleeing northwards, when the end comes. Yet they contribute in their way to the tragedy: stirring up political hopes of a nationalist revolt, against Jesus' will, and then deserting him when their bumbling backfires. Judas seems to be slightly more purposeful, but only slightly so. He acts in a definite way; nevertheless he acts in confusion and, to judge by his own outcome, aimlessness. The Romans perform the actual execution, yet this too is purposeless, since Pilate knows that there is no real merit in the charges of sedition. The Jews claim responsibility for the death, yet the very mob that is so sure he should be liquidated is the same that hurrahed him into their city brief days before. Theirs is even greater confusion. It is Jesus who is purposeful about his death, who has seen it coming, accepts it as inevitable, and yields a life which he refuses to lead in any other way. But the Gospel's deepest insight is that Jesus' Father had intended his death from the first, and proposed all along to raise him then to new life, and others after him, so that men might be reconciled to Him. It is this insistence on the priority of God's plan which is a constant theme in the Gospel, and one of its most effective ways of expressing divine grace. This initiative, which theologians sometimes call prevenience, invests the whole of the Gospel account.

A literary tradition somewhat younger than the passion narrative is the gospel of Jesus' ministry. Here, too, there is strong emphasis on Jesus' purposefulness. He is basically an itinerant preacher. He heals the sick and he talks of repentance. In either case Jesus is said to be led by the Spirit of his Father. And preaching and healing form a single mission: to bring life to men who are limp and listless. His healing is the introduction and illustration of his word, which is all about unsolicited service to one's needy neighbor. It is clear, as the story moves on, that Jesus is in opposition to the religion of the land. And clear also that everyone has plans for him, but that he evades them all to continue what he had from the first decided upon: to seek men out and to rally them to his life-giving mission. Once again, he is a man of purpose, of prevenience, of grace.

The latest portion of the Gospel to be created is that which purports to describe his infancy, while in reality dealing with his origins behind time. The gospel, growing chronologically through its editorial history, is first concerned with the events of that final weekend; later interest moves backward in reminiscence over his public career; finally it speculates on his identity prior to his appearance. Thus the Gospel first fastens its interest upon a moment, then moves backward through a period of time, and finally lets its concern break out of time entirely.

The infancy gospels never really dwell on his family origins, which were either unknown or obscure or in any case uninteresting, but on Jesus' role as one sent into history to fulfill eternal plans. Here it is that grace is most strongly asserted: the Father destined his Son before Abraham was, to join the sons of men. All that had happened in Israel, and indeed since Adam, was coiled within a prior purpose. The inference of Jesus' pre-existence is not a dry doctrinal statement, but an affirmation of grace, in the Father's generosity being anterior to all human hopes or performance. If Jesus is divine, then he is utterly prior to all men's affairs. If there is talk of an eternal mystery, a surprise which the Father holds in store for men in the final era, then this precisely underlines how men are like sparrows in his hand.

There is nothing very astonishing about a God who loves us relentlessly, save that we generally do not believe in one. The hope of this book is to examine what differences such a belief would make to our doctrine, our ethic, and our ritual, which have too often been directed to a god of whom we have really, at heart, been warily and cautiously afraid.

And what difference would such belief, such a God, make for Philemon? So many persons press in upon him as he deliberates about his slave. He would somehow do a kindness to Onesimus, placate Paul, keep his other slaves submissive, maintain his family estate, offer the most magnanimous example to his comrades in faith, and retain the trust of his fellow slaveowners in the neighborhood—all at once. But he cannot do justice to all these claims. If he yields to the most insistent, he chooses what is expedient. If he seeks to do justice as best he can, he chooses to be ethical. If, however, he consider himself not so much plagued by impossibly competing needs, as haunted by a God whose love comes at him with relentless and incredible generosity, then he will burst out of the muddle. Decision, not really forced by the issue itself, is summoned from him by another call. Philemon's life is energized, not simply by the moral situations he faces, but by his own inward character, which is driven beyond what is just to what will release the intensest response of love to the Father. Philemon's God would stir any believer to incalculable lengths.

2 His Father's Son, Firstborn of Many Brethren

A principal disclosure of Christianity is the unyielding love of God the Father. As was pointed out, Christians find this about as unbelievable as do others, yet it is this God whom we are charged to preach. Much more before our eyes, however, is Jesus of Nazareth his Son, a man among us, flesh of our flesh and bone of our bone. It is in seeing Jesus that we catch our best glimpse of the Father whom we cannot see. It is one of Jesus' Jewish titles, Messiah (= Christ) that has given our particular church its name. Yet Jesus the Christ (and the God he embodies) cannot be rightly understood until we clear up one very grievous and ancient misunderstanding. What I wish to argue in this chapter is that it is *not* the peculiar and exclusive mission of Jesus to save men.

Much conventional Christian preaching, on the other hand, pleads that all men are saved through Jesus. The claim might best be understood in the context of what we might call the "savior myth,"[1] which is also commonly accepted

---

[1] I do not employ the term "myth" here in its derogatory sense, as a tale of the affairs of pagan gods. I intend its other sense: a story told of God's relations with men which, simple as a parable, captures some particular point of the mystery.

and put abroad by believers. This is a myth that is rarely
recounted in few words, but can easily be reconstructed from
catechisms the world over, though it may take on a slightly
different turn or flavor in this or that locality. It runs basically thus: In the beginning God created man good; man was
at peace with the Creator and with his fellows. Through some
primeval sin man rejected a divine command, and was punished by being left to his quarrelsome self in an appropriately
antagonistic environment. This spirit of disobedience was
passed on from parents to children almost like a hereditary
curse. Human affairs went from bad to worse as men perpetrated ever new outrages upon one another. Yet, even as he
turned in anger from his rebellious creatures, in his heart of
hearts God hankered to have him back, and slowly prepared
the way for a reconciliation. His only Son became man himself, and since he brought into human flesh that perfect obedience of Son to Father, he lived without sin even through
violent death. At last there was one man who justly earned
the Father's good pleasure. In rewarding him the Father not
only exalted him as man into the glory of his native intimacy
with himself, but for his sake turned his face once again
towards all men who would associate themselves with Jesus
his Son, would receive the graces of salvation earned by
Jesus' passion, and would live in the same final subjection
that had marked his life. The gates of heaven were once more
opened in welcome, and salvation offered to all who would
believe in Jesus Christ as Son of God.

This little salvation history, however it is narrated, stum-
bles in several directions. To begin with, the character of God
as described is curiously inconsistent. If God does turn from
man in wrath, how serious can it be if he is all the time
planning to undo the disaster? If he is benevolent enough to
hand over his only Son to death, what need does he really
have to be appeased? Is atonement carried out just for the
sake of protocol? You must either take God to be radically
alienated by sinful man, in which case the Savior could hard-

ly come under his Father's auspices, or believe in a God who is not really wrathful, only sullen enough to pout for a few millenia, in which case the atonement would seem to be a way of truckling up to his injured feelings. Neither God has much appeal.

Secondly, if Jesus' death and resurrection were the necessary prerequisites to salvation, what of the vast throngs of men born and dead before the event? Are so many thousands of generations of Adam's children excluded from grace because born out of due time? Theologians have speculated that grace was in fact made available to them by a sort of Keynesian deficit spending on God's part: he advanced his grace in anticipation of Jesus' accomplishment. But aside from this unfortunate economic metaphor that debases the God-man relationship to a commercial transaction, no hopeful or satisfying explanation is offered why the Savior, coming quite late into history, leaves behind so many brethren. And indeed, if salvation is given by faith in Christ, there is the further problem that the Christian message has never been heard by more than a small minority of those who have lived after the event, nor can one reasonably presume that it is ever going to be otherwise.[2] How bent upon saving men can God really be if the event touches but very few?

The real objection to this makeshift Christian myth, however, is that it is basically blasphemous. It glorifies Jesus by discrediting his Father. It denies precisely what Jesus has disclosed about the Father: that he never turns away from man no matter how much man may turn from him, that he has no moods or temper, and cannot be provoked or offended. The flaw in the myth is that it is one more device adopted by men who cannot quite bring themselves to believe that there is a God who loves with an unyielding love. They must

---

[2]See the excellent essay by Karl Rahner, "A Theological Interpretation of the Position of Christians in the Modern World," in *Mission and Grace*, trans. Cecily Hastings (New York: Sheed and Ward, 1963), I, 3-55.

somehow imagine him turning away, and needing to be reconciled by some appropriate event upon earth. The fact that
the Savior is himself the divine Son become man does not
purge the myth of this inconsistent but antichristian suggestion that there had to be at least one utterly virtuous man to
justify a restoration of God's love for mankind.

If what Jesus conveys about his Father is true, then his
benevolence knows no seasons. His grace is perpetual; the full
complex of his gift-giving to men can never be intermittent.
There can be no temporary suspension of grace, understood
either as the Father's favorful attitude, or as its saving effects
in men. In brief, there can be no history of salvation, if by
that one intends that God's grace is first interdicted in time,
and then made available once more because of Jesus' accomplishments. Jesus, then, can in no exclusive or particular way
be our Savior.

Why the Need for Israel, or Jesus, or Church?

What, then, is he? The particular purpose for which the Son
was sent was precisely to reveal to men that there is a God
who is always saving, to disclose that the Father has no
wrath, that he unleashes his gratuity upon all men no matter
what their condition. At all times and in all places the Father
is at work, touching the hearts of men to draw them from
selfishness into love. Before Abraham was. . .further than the
word of the gospel can reach. . .there is the Father at work.
Or, to put it in other terms, the visible mission of Jesus,
which (understood as comprising its preliminaries in Israel
and its follow-up in Christianity) is a phenomenon in history
and is a limited, particular movement among men, is not
nearly so universal as the invisible mission of the Spirit,
whereby God reaches out to all men in history.

Jesus' revelation is not only an insight into his Father.
He also discloses how, though God cannot turn from us, we

can and do turn from him. By his death for those who slay him, Jesus displays their own evil to those who have eyes to see. The alienation, then, is on our part, and it is not God who must be transformed, but ourselves.

Jesus does not come to perform before God; he comes to call us—by revealing to us the character of his Father, and that of ourselves. The actual work of saving men, of purifying them from sin and drawing them into love, has gone on unremittingly as long as there have been men. But our understanding of this was given a jolt of transforming insight in the coming of Jesus Christ. In this sense Jesus is better understood as Revealer, than as Savior.

The little myth which has embodied this theology is admittedly as much folk tale as it is dogma, but it is in such folk forms of belief that religion has its most unguarded and telltale moments. As for the tale, if heaven has gates—and walls and locks and the other foreboding symbols of aloofness—then the Father of Jesus does not live there. It is curious how Christians do confess him to be radically gracious, yet falter when it comes to believing that he should be entirely so.

This same hesitation also shows itself in other folkways. There is, for example, the folk tale, or myth, of Mary. A man died and went to heaven to seek admittance. St. Peter checked his credentials at the gateway, but the record was very bad and he was told to go to hell. He appealed. When Christ came to the entry to render judgment his aspect was far more severe and forbidding than Peter's. The man was very definitely sent on his way. In despair and bewilderment the man wandered around the circuit of the walls for one last, wistful look, when the back door opened and a very motherly woman emerged. She asked him why he looked so woebegone. When he told his story, her heart was moved with motherly pity. Taking him by the hand she drew him inside, and went off to speak a word in his favor to her Son. The

Son, who could never be severe with his own mother, agreed to relent for her poor friend. And thus one more sinner was welcomed into the kingdom.

The point of the story, of course, is that in the popular Christian mind God is not nearly as approachable or as compassionate as human beings. Over the centuries Jesus of Nazareth has been progressively divinized; what this means is that, in inverse proportion, he has been bleached of his humanity. The more he was focused back into the remote inaccessiblity of the Lord, the more Christianity has resorted to mediation by Mary and the saints. Over recent centuries, it is noteworthy that most visionaries in the Catholic tradition have been having visions, not of Jesus Christ, but of his mother: a more familiar person, more welcoming, easier to converse with. The cult of the saints, moreover, both in biography and in worship, suggests that believers turn to them (or to romanticized images of them) as congenial—even homely—and well-connected advocates who are willing to act as go-betweens with the Lord, who does not himself listen to sinners. There seems to be a similar persuasion behind the theological movement in our time which would insist that Jesus was far more human than is generally thought, that he knew all the anguish and bewilderment of any prophet faced with violent death, that he suffered the same weaknesses and temptations and failures that we are commonly subject to, that he had a human father like all men. Thus, it is felt, he will be more *sympathique,* more approachable, more reassuring, because more human. Unfortunately, acceptance of man in his weakness is not seen as a very divine quality.

I, for one, would find Jesus far more reassuring if he did not have my faults and foibles which make me untrustworthy. But the issue is this: to the extent that this folk-view influences the Christian mind, to the extent that to be divine is seen effectively as being inferior to being human, the incarnation has failed. What the very adventure of the Son in our man-flesh strives to convey is that there is a welcoming love, an unconditioned acceptance, a relentless and eternal affection in the Father which so far exceeds our own experience that even the selfless career and death of Jesus can only hint at it. The very substance of our faith is the belief and hope that behind this hint lies love beyond measure.

As for mediation, it is not we who must resort to go-betweens in order to approach a difficult and intractable God, but he who must use all manner of intermediaries to break through the aloofness of a stiff-necked and blind people. If there is alienation, it is we who turn away from him and withdraw. If anyone is inaccessible, it is not God but man in his egoism. Our hearts are no mystery to him; it is his heart that we find either uninteresting or incredible. The whole thrust of mediation comes from him to us, as God's self-disclosure breaks through our all-too-human nonchalance.

If, then, the Father of Jesus cannot but love men, he is perforce at work unremittingly in the world, reconciling men to himself, whether or not they be aware of him. The mission of Israel/Jesus Christ/the Church is *to reveal* that there is such a saving God. The work of salvation is universal; the work of revelation is historically limited. Furthermore, it is not necessary. With or without the incarnation the Father's work would inexorably continue. Jesus' coming is not a necessity: it is a luxury, a grace, an abundance of bounty. What is absolutely crucial to man is that he be saved: that through God's grace he become a loving person. If, in addition, he also discovers that this is of eternal significance, so much the better for him. As I shall later contend, revelation is itself most powerfully contributory to salvation. But these are nonetheless separable and often separate realities.

Salvation Beyond Church

That so many fail to see this is probably due to Paul and Augustine. They were the two most influential writers on

grace in the Christian tradition. Each underwent a violent
change in the course of his life through a dramatic conversion
experience. Both later looked back on their preconversion
days with considerable shame—one feels that there may have
been some unrealistic exaggeration in the way they vilified
their own respective days of youth. And because for each of
them the moment of conversion involved a shattering revelation that drew them out of their former depravity into belief
in Christ and baptism into the Church, each of them took his
own experience to be the paradigm of what every man must
undergo. For both Paul and Augustine the salvation event
coincided with revelation; thereafter they naturally failed to
notice the distinction.

Thus under their aegis the Christian tradition has considered that all non-Christians are depraved sinners, and that
faith and baptism are the only avenue of salvation. Extrapolating still further, they have writ this large over the history of mankind, and argued that before the release of salvific grace in Christ, all men wallowed in sin, as a *massa
damnata*. Paul, in refuting the Judaizers, and Augustine in his
arguments with the Pelagians, both tried to establish the prevenience of God's grace by seeing it as having a sort of chron-
ological priority. Both individual and race, they said, pass
through an early stage of depravity, and what saves them
from it is Christ: in his death and resurrection for the race, in
faith and baptism for the individual. Both Paul and Augustine
are so earnestly anxious to share their own life-giving experience with others—like recent returnees from a weekend of
sensitivity training—that they give little thought to the possibility—indeed, the inevitability—that God has other, more co-
vert but equally powerful ways of converting men who have
never heard of Christ.

It was Cyprian of Carthage, Augustine's predecessor in
that North African town by almost two centuries, who is
credited with having put it most bluntly: "*Extra ecclesiam
nulla salus:* There is no salvation outside the Church". Both

the formula and the idea behind it have clung to the Christian mind ever since.

The activity which most brings this to the fore, of course, is missionary work. Francis Xavier, the saintly Jesuit who introduced Christianity to vast areas of India, Ceylon, China, and Japan is not untypical in his attitudes. At Malindi, he had had some contact with Islam which he regarded as loathsome.

> The Moors were edified by seeing how we Christians lay our dead to rest. One of them, a man highly respected in the city, asked me whether our churches were much frequented, and if our people prayed with fervour. He said that devotion had declined markedly among his own community, and wondered if the same thing had happened to the Christians. . .He could not understand why there had been such a serious falling-off in devotion, and gave as his opinion that it must have resulted from some great sin. We argued the point a long while, but he was not satisfied with my solution, that God, the all-faithful, abided not with infidels and took no pleasure in their prayers.[3]

Contempt for the infidel surely had much to do with the brutality used by the early Christian Conquistadores, who easily adopted the view of Joâo de Barros, that "though the Moors and Gentiles are certainly rational creatures and so potential converts to Christianity, yet since they show no disposition to be converted, we Christians have no duties towards them."[4]

Xavier grew very attached to one ship's captain, a Chi-

---

[3]James Brodrick, S.J., *St. Francis Xavier* (New York: The Wicklow Press, 1952), pp. 107-108.

[4]*Ibid.*, p. 117.

nese, who conducted him through some very dangerous wa-
ters and proved a more trustworthy comrade than most of
the profiteering, Christian Portuguese sailors.

They were brothers under the skin, both of
them kindly and daring souls, though in different
fashions, and but for that execrable idol (kept by
the captain) they might have been the best of
friends. Before the year was out, Francis wrote
from Japan to Dom Pedro da Silva to say that poor
Ladrâo was dead. "All through the voyage," he
continued, "he was good to us, and we were unable
to be good to him, for he died in his infidelity.
Even after death we could not help him by our
prayers to God, for his soul was in Hell."[5]

Such an arrogant theology would, when confided to a great
and holy man like Xavier, simply blind him to some of the
good and godliness that he confronted every day. In the
hands of the Portuguese adventurers and other Christian ex-
plorers, traders, theologians, and soldiers, it would under-
write all manner of savagery and contempt, and cause the
spread of European influence to disparage and smother flour-
ishing cultures and gentle men in all corners of the earth.

Attitudes in latter years have softened. Whether from a
feeling of fair play, or camaraderie, or just simple good sense,
Christians are no longer anxious to consign all heathens to
hell. Integrating this attitude into their theology has not
been all that easy, however. To please the theologians, the
salvation of the unbeliever has in some adequately technical
way to be brought in under church auspices. Thus, one
speaks of "baptism of desire": those who are virtuously disposed, yet through no fault of their own do not know about
their obligation to become Christians, are deemed to be as if

[5]*Ibid.*, p. 357.

they had been baptized. They are sometimes called "crypto-Christians", which would have irritated men like Gandhi, who was not at all ignorant about either Christ or Christians, and had no desire to join them. Theologians talk about a sort of associate membership in the Church, an affiliation unwittingly enjoyed by all men of good will.

Shortly after World War II Leonard Feeney, a Boston Jesuit, became rather obsessive and articulate in support of the old dictum, *Extra ecclesiam nulla salus*. This he construed quite literally: only official members of the Roman Catholic Church can be saved. That is probably just what St. Cyprian had in mind, and many others who endorsed the doctrine down the centuries. But modern views are more tolerant, if also more muddled, and Father Feeney soon found himself, for all his loyalty, *extra ecclesiam* by bell, book, and candle.

It is time for the Church bluntly to disavow Cyprian's maxim, and to admit that *extra ecclesiam* there is plenty of *salus*. This need be no grudging admission. It is the very commission the Church has received: to publicize that God's effective love knows no bounds. The Christian Church can claim no bonded franchise for salvation, no exclusive rights of distributorship for God's grace. It is perhaps one of the rare religious enterprises that confesses it is not necessary. It calls attention, not to itself, but to a Father who is already reconciling men to himself. As the roadside signs say: "Jesus saves". But so do many others, all by enablement of the same Father. The Church is to reveal, to publicize to all men by service and preaching—and to its members further through worship—that there is a God who loves us beyond imagining. Membership in the Church signifies a response: belief in the good news, and a commitment to love beyond measure. The Church is not the assembly of the saved; it is the assembly of those who know that there is a saving God.

Obviously I speak of what should be, rather than what really is. The Church's continual failure to carry out the terms of its original warrant has led it into two misfortunes.

First of all, what Christians preach is often bad news, not good. Approaching their fellows with the presumption that they are all reprobate, they arrogantly offer them (on terms) a way out of their sinfulness. But the Christian can make no legitimate presumptions about any man. He has good news to offer anyone: to sinners that they be encouraged to repent; to the righteous that they learn how they are so and how much more so they might be.

The Church cannot meet the world armed only with condemnation. For many men there must on the contrary be enthusiastic congratulation: "You are doing what we speak of!" When a stranger is seen to be living for his neighbor, to be spending himself on others in their need, the gospel is meant to encounter him not with blame but with commendation: He is living in grace. The Christian comes not just to tear down and to uproot, but to build and to plant. Too much woe has come from our coming at men with eyes shut and mouth open, bent on gifting grace to a graceless world.

There is a further misfortune. By fancying itself as God's unique channel of salvation, the Church inevitably degenerates into institutional egotism. Clerics tend to fret about Church membership, and attendance at services, and "vocation" trends, losing sight of the more substantial signs of the growth or decline of human compassion, or wisdom, or welfare, which are the really telltale indices of grace in the world. To have the Church as one's overriding concern is so stale. The Church's main task is not to spread the Church; it is to spread faith and love and service. Men who heed the message will coagulate and group into the Church, but this is not the purpose: it is a by-product. The Church is not sent into the world with an uncommon work to do. It is sent with an uncommon insight from revelation to join in a most common work: salvation.

Here one is reminded that Jesus was curiously unpreoccupied about the future of those who believed through him. His attention went rather to those who were deprived:

to the running sores of the leper; to the milky, sightless eye; to the dragging, withered leg; to the slack-mouthed village idiot; to the shrunken belly; even to the dead man in his grave. With all these he shared out life as they had need. To those other deprived, who had no need, he gave harsh warning that if they did not share their substance with brothers in need, then they were even more dreadfully lifeless. Yet for his disciples, he had little care and few words. They were to follow him, joining in the work. His day was spent facing those who did not believe: working for them, speaking to them. As for the believers, they were more taken for granted: he did not face them, but expected them to be at his side, giving the same work and word. In the evening, perhaps when supper had given way to a weary reverie around the fire, he might turn to them with a few words.

Left to themselves, they set about organizing. He reacted impatiently, likened them to heathen princes contending for power. Let them imitate slaves and servants, he said, and more work would get done. Some have concluded that Jesus had no intention of founding a Church. A wiser observation would be that he had no illusions about how to found one. His consuming desire was spent in walking about, doing the work and spreading the word. Those who believed would fall in step behind him, and thus a Church was formed in his wake: but it was only his Church as long as it faced and moved with him, and did not turn inward upon itself. His followers might well organize as groups do, and this one quickly did: with officers and laws, fiscal resources and approved rituals and the other provisions men commonly make to preserve the purpose and integrity of their enterprises as they pass into the waiting hands of generations that follow Israel had all this. Jesus' kingdom, however, is assured and assembled, not by such Church organization, but by individual conversion. For this one cannot organize. Though men are sometimes converted in groups, no group was ever converted. The heart of man is touched and healed most personally by the finger of God. Only individuals are converted. Only individuals are holy. Only individuals love or believe. Thus, if Jesus' work of revelation and salvation is continued, there will be a Church. But the mere fact that the Church is continued gives no guarantee that Jesus' mission will be continued.

Before going forward, let me recapitulate. Jesus embodies for us a Father who loves us even when we fail to love. Thus though we are easily turned away from him, he remains steadfastly turned towards us. We do not deal directly with God, but in reacting to our neighbor we are, under it all, reacting to the Father. Salvation occurs whenever any man emerges from his native selfishness and opens his heart to his neighbor. This change of heart is verified and embodied in service of fellowman. Now this goes on everywhere, yet not simply on our own strength, for we are not to the manner born. We begin very much wrapped up in ourselves, and for us to turn our concern and our goods and our whole life towards our neighbor requires that God enable us to do it. This we call a favor, a grace. And grace, like bacteria, is everywhere. God loves all men, favoring them at all times and drawing them into his love, wittingly or unwittingly. Grace is no monopoly of Christianity. The Church has been given no franchise on God's favor. The unbeliever and the believer are saved in exactly the same way: by loving and serving their neighbor. The difference is that the believer has been alerted 'to the fact that in this transaction eternity is at stake.

The purpose of Jesus is to save men, and his particular way of doing this is not simply to touch them with his generosity, but to reveal that this is an intimation of what God is like. The Church is to continue this: to join the universal, human work of bringing men to life, and to reveal that all that passes between men affects their relationship to God. Unlike almost all religions, Christianity has no special set of actions which provide a short-cut around or a remedy for the day-to-day transactions men have between themselves. Christianity, instead, fastens deeper attention on these crucial, non-religious activities.

It is not only that religion runs the perpetual risk of hypocrisy, but that religion is not the substance of salvation. When Jesus himself talks about how men will fare beyond death, it is noteworthy that religion in no way comes into the discussion. In the parable of judgment, in Matthew 25, Jesus infers that men will be judged neither by their religious fidelity nor by the specific religious commandments of Israel. They will be judged on whether or not they have fed, housed, clothed, refreshed, healed, or consoled their neighbor in need. Elsewhere he dwells on like themes: he talks of taking in the orphans from the streets, providing a home for the widow who has neither family nor food, burying the bodies that are left to rot, caring for the people with contagious diseases. The very things Jesus preaches are in no way religious. He is constantly drawing attention away from ritual activities, from religion, from what is specifically intra-church, to the secular, material service of neighbor in need. Thus the purpose of religion is to lead men to salvation, but not to replace these salvific acts with others of its own making.

Why, then, the Church?

The only place one can find the Father is in one's brother, and in the transaction of goods and services which will help that brother to become nourished and to grow. If this be so, the Church dare not offer its own activities as a short-circuit around one's neighbor. There are no direct transactions with the Father: no one has ever seen God. And the only words which we can speak to him with sincerity are the words that are verified by our dealings with our brother. No man can love the Father whom he does not see, without loving the brother whom he does see.

Thus, the most crucial activities of Christians are not peculiar to Christians. Christianity must be dedicated to what is not particular to Christianity. It must be a most outward-facing group. It must be an agency of service, with the understanding that in washing the feet of the world, one is doing far more than would appear. What marks this agency of service is the conviction of those who serve that they are responding to the boundless love of the Father, and are drawing others to respond, whether or not they believe. Yet what marks this agency of service off from others is less important than what it shares in common with all service. Faith, precious as it is, is something we can do without (indeed, at the end of time, Paul notes, it will evaporate along with hope); love is something no one can do without.

Not too long ago a bill was introduced into the Oregon legislature, intended to remove tax exemption from athletic associations, churches, and fraternal lodges, meanwhile reaffirming the exemptions granted to orphanages, hospitals, and similar institutions. The bill was defeated, but what is perhaps more significant is that a good number of legislators felt that they should draw the line between those organizations that serve themselves and those which serve others. It was very clear to them on which side of that line the churches fell. Their observation should strike the churches as a devastating accusation and a call to return to their proper purpose. The Church must be an organization that serves the unfortunate, acting in the belief that its service must be revelatory as the service of Jesus was. Its purpose goes beyond the secular succoring of neighbor; it is the conveyance to neighbor of more than bread alone, in the belief that whenever man gives bread in love, he does not give bread alone.

Despite the apparently negative tone of this chapter, it is not intended as one more angry (and tedious) philippic against the Church. But if Jesus is our Lord, then it is our business to seek his kingdom as he did. We do this first of all by giving life and its supports to those who have it in short measure; that life is love. Further, we try to share our secret: that it is only in serving our brother that we are reconciled to our Father, who loves us and calls us to himself. Revelation, though unnecessary, is a most precious grace, which has no purpose but to contribute to our salvation.

Still, some will feel, the Church does not then seem all that important. I often believe that this complaint arises most from those churchmen who, leaving little trace of any real contribution to this world, must prop up their self-esteem with the illusion that they must be important to have around. Yet taking the query at face-value, we might put it into its bluntest terms: what real gain does faith afford the man who is already living through grace in love? Why need the Church bother someone who is already saved? In reply I would offer a story, an awkward parable of my own making. It concerns a man called Joe.

Joe was the very brilliant son of a working-class family: his father was an unskilled worker at the city fish market. With eight other children to support, he was in no position to finance Joe's college education (nor, in the pre-welfare-state days of our story, was the government with cash forthcoming). Thus, upon finishing high school Joe expected to begin working his way up through the echelons of employment at the fish market. That summer, however, his father took him aside to tell him that, unknown to Joe, his parents had been laying money aside for his education, and could stake him to a first year at college. With equal surprise and zest Joe enrolled at the university, and his mind grew and strengthened as the wisdom of great men became his. Each year his father slipped him another envelope, and Joe was a son to be proud of. He was especially interested in philosophy and sociology, and when he graduated he yearned to learn more about the way men live closely together in cities. The parental support was still available, and Joe obtained a doctorate in urban studies at the finest graduate school in the country. With his new young wife he took his first job in the

planning department of Smokestack, Indiana, and there the
full force of his talents and his great-hearted desire to serve
became apparent. The city bloomed under his touch. Ghet-
toes were deftly transformed into lovely family neighbor-
hoods; traffic somehow flowed more smoothly; the chimneys
of the mills left no more misery hanging darkly in the air; the
schools were upgraded, integrated, and served as examples for
educationists all over the country. In a word, Joe gave his
best to Smokestack and the vision and forcefulness of the
man brought hope and delight to a people that had once lived
in blight.

One evening, while Joe was relaxing at home with his
wife and children, an elderly man knocked at the door. He
hesitantly introduced himself as someone who had lived
down the street during Joe's youth; Joe admitted that his
face was vaguely familiar, but apologized that he had had a
young boy's neglect of older folk on the street. The neglect,
however, had not been mutual. "I don't really know why I
stopped by," explained the old man, "but I have a great
interest in you. I saw that you were the brightest boy in the
neighborhood, and knew also that your folks wouldn't be
able to help you through college. I had more money than I
knew what to do with, yet I knew your family had a pride of
its own, so every year I sent your father an unmarked envelope with $3,000 inside, and was confident that your father
would want to use it for you. I have followed your growth
and your career, and simply wanted to come and tell you
finally how proud I am of you, and how pleased I am that
my contribution has brought such renewal through your
hands to this city."

Now what does the arrival of this man at Joe's door
bring to him? Joe is already, through this man's unknown
generosity, a highly resourceful and generous man who
spends himself for his neighbor. Yet what a gift the encounter is for Joe! He is overcome at discovering this man who had
loved him when he knew nothing of it, and would not for the

world have missed learning the truth. The revelation is a disclosure to him that he has been loved in an incomparable way, and he turns to the man in gratitude, and to his wife and children and Smokestack with an even higher dedication, for he is more deeply convinced than ever that it is only the sharing of life among men that makes one rich. The joy of the revelation, though it overflows into his work, has a value that escapes measure.[6]

So it is that for any man, no matter how noble and self-giving and courageous, the discovery that Jesus of Nazareth has died for him speaks to his heart and wreaks a deep transformation. For some, it might be inaccurate to speak of a conversion, but the discovery of being loved beyond our imagining, without our knowing it has the power to touch our deepest heart, and change our life so mightily that the best of men will speak of it as if they had been struck down in mid-journey and had their eyes opened, as if they had been blind before.

[6]Paul Horgan develops a theme not unlike that in my story in his splendid novel, *Whitewater* (New York: Farrar, Straus and Giroux, 1970).

3 A Disquieting Ethic

The earliest two chapters of this book inquired into one of the insights in the New Testament which we took to be indispensable, and pursued the clues it offered for understanding the character of God and the purposes of Jesus, his Son. These two chapters to follow will turn, now, from doctrine to ethics, from systematic to moral theology. Immediately we stumble onto a problem. If, taking Jesus as an embodiment of the Father, we believe that God is love, that he relentlessly cherishes and accepts us; if he can be neither pleased nor offended, since our behavior is no motive for his love: then what need have we of ethics? If he has a welcome for us whether we keep his commandments or not, why bother with them?

Indeed, quite apart from the particular theology we are trying to elaborate, commandments have not been very well received by many recent theologians. The world, we are told, has recently come of age—during the imprisonment of Dietrich Bonhöffer, it is said—and can no longer depend upon childish contrivance or priestly deceit. The theologians are not complaining simply about the laws of Moses. Their objection goes much deeper, to the very notion of commandment: any precept that presumes, in our immensely complex and unpredictable world, to say in advance what is right and what wrong. General guidelines, folk wisdom, experienced advice: yes, they might offer some small help. But there can be no commandments, it is said, no absolute and abstract prescriptions to tell men in advance how to behave in trying situations.

There is much to be said in favor of commandments. Basically, they are one of the forms whereby the benefits of human experience and moral reflection can be made available to future generations. They are, in fact, one of the better ways to do this. In most societies the only effective way moral wisdom can be made publicly available is through law. Most men would give no notice at all to the subtle inquiries of Plato, Amen-em-ope, Lucretius, or Boethius, yet would heed the same ethical insights if they came on the say-so of Alexander of Macedon, the Son-God Amon, emperor Theodosius, or even the local priest. Priests have always had a closer sense of popular needs and minds than have theologians. Hence even within the Christian tradition churchmen have preferred to give commands (whether in God's name or in their own) rather than to tolerate ambiguity. Justice will more surely be done when ordered by authority than when argued for by wise men. The ruler may use a language different from the sage, but both try to pass on moral wisdom.

Another criticism of commandments is that they are so complex and petty. All legal systems tend to gather detail as they go along, to proliferate and to grow in number and complexity of statutes. The rule of law, it appears, becomes more and more burdensome and inhibiting. But this may be a hasty criticism, particularly in the Judeo-Christian tradition. As we observed in the first chapter, most gods tend to come across as mysterious, powerful, and demanding. Man's primal reaction to such an awesome god is fear, even terror. God's expectations are so impossible to reckon, his displeasure hard to anticipate, his anger so disastrous. In this context, the disclosure of commandments would be more a rescue than a burden. It was surely seen so in Israel. Knowing what the Lord demanded was a remedy for fear, a clear advantage over the pagans. Of course, to know commandments is not to keep them. Still, guilt from sin seemed less fearsome than the dread of not knowing Yahweh's paths. Thus the Torah was a gift, a delight. Its very complexity, the web of legalisms that were spun around it long before the Jewish rabbis or Christian divines enwrapped it in their later cocoons of casuistry was in the believer's favor: even in extraordinary eventualities one could know exactly what God wanted done.

A commandment is one of several possible kinds of moral discourse. Some writers today argue that it is preferable and more mature to say, "This is good," than to say, "Thou shalt do this". But really, every imperative statement ultimately resolves inself into a declarative one. When a father forbids his son to sleep round the town, he is really warning him that if he does, he will offend social custom, or incur a paternity suit, or get the clap, or be disinherited, or hurt some girl, or go to hell, or become an insensitive and loveless man. Even in the case where the father backs up his command with his own threat of sanction, he is still warning the son of evil, just as surely as if he used the straightforward language of advice instead of command.

Moral law is a form of tradition. One suspects that much of the present impatience with commandments in the Church is not simply a rejection of authority or of imperatives, but a distrust of the experience and moral reflection of earlier times. Particularly now when culture is abruptly tossed into upheaval, sons naturally discount their fathers' advice, whatever form it takes. Sadly, these may be the times when tradition is most needed.

Commandments, then, are one way of sharing exper-

ience with those to come. But they do leave much to be
desired. The New Testment is ill at ease with commandments
as a form of moral discourse, and I should like to propose
that its grievance with law is one the Church today should
heed.

Hebrew law has roots reaching back to the time of the
exodus and conquest. After invading Canaan, the clans
settled in scattered pockets throughout the territory. The
task of settling disputes between tribes and tribesmen, easily
accomplished by the central leader during the old nomad
days, now fell to the local chiefs. By a combination of shrewd
folk wisdom and the throwing of magical lots they saw that
justice was done and the peace maintained. In time, landmark
decisions came to be publicized and remembered. There was
the time, for instance, when an engaged girl was caught *in
flagrante delicto,* but claimed she had been raped. Not so,
said the elder: she was in the village, and could always have
let out a couple of good shrieks. Had she been in the country-
side with no one to hear, the presumption would be in her
favor, and the judgment would lean towards assault. The
sentence: both parties to be stoned to death (Deuteronomy
22, 23-27).

There was another famous case of the ox that gored to
death another ox in a neighboring pasture. The usual arrange-
ment was that the surviving ox would be sold, the two owners to share the proceeds and also divide the carcass of the
dead ox between them. But in this case the goring ox had
been known to be vicious (there had been other incidents),
yet was never fenced in or tied properly. The verdict: the live
ox was forfeited to the dead animals's owner, since the inci-
dent involved criminal negligence; the careless owner was left
with the dead animal (Exodus 21, 35-36).

As the memory of particularly wise decisions accumu-
lated into common law, each new case no longer needed to
be resolved merely by the local elder's ingenuity; increasingly
he could and would invoke precedent. When these precedents

became codified, they were transformed from narrative (for example, the story of Solomon's judgment between the two disputing harlots is still in this form) into imperative. By being cast into the format of legislation, rather than that of judicial precedent, they were given enhanced authority. In more ancient days justice had been decided mostly by divination and by lot. The result was thus attributed to God and accepted without rebellion. As human judgment first augmented and then replaced magic, it had to be grounded on comparable authority. This was first done by tracing the legitimacy of the local elder-judges to Moses (Exodus 19, 13-25; Deuteronomy 1, 9-18; 16, 18-20). Later, when the common law was converted to writing, their decisions were converted to commandments. They were no longer known as the judgments of shrewd men. They were, by literary convention, put into the mouth of Moses; they became the Word of the Lord himself. And they were thereby the better kept.

Yet the strength of the system was a fragile strength. As long as the people lacked any developed historical sense, they would think that the commandments were not the work of a human judicial tradition, but imagine that they were delivered by God directly. Such a code, particularly when committed to writing, could have a stupefying effect upon the needs of an ongoing tradition.

One way the moral tradition preserved its needed suppleness was by supplementing the Torah with a continuous oral interpretation. Young scribes were educated at the feet of elder rabbis, asking them questions and being quizzed in return. The anecdote about Jesus staying in the temple as a youth suggests just this sort of teacher-disciple interchange that can still be seen in the Moslem tradition. It combines a retention of the ancient texts by memory with a personal flair for making further casuistic applications.

The New Testament builds upon this base. When John came baptizing, for example, his message was a call to repentance. Luke mentions that various classes of people approached him with questions that called for the usual sort of rabbinical answers.

> When all the people asked him, "What must we do, then?" he answered, "If anyone has two tunics he must share with the man who has none, and the one with something to eat must do the same". There were tax collectors too who came for baptism, and these said to him, "Master, what must we do?" He said to them, "Exact no more than your rate". Some soldiers asked him in their turn, "What about us? What must we do?" He said to them, "No intimidation! No extortion! Be content with your pay!" (3, 10-14)

The questions put to John were the standard queries addressed to any rabbi, particularly one of a reformist persuasion: how should one lead his life righteously in the sight of the Lord? His answers are in the highest tradition of Israel. What he enjoins is the highest equity, and the relinquishing of self-aggrandizement in the face of a neighbor's deprivation.

Inadequacy of Commandments

But as soon as we examine the ethical injunctions of Jesus, we see a sharply different approach, the beginning of a new moral tradition that finds law an inadequate medium for its conveyance. Compare the anecdote about John, recounted above, with the reply of Jesus to virtually the same sort of questions.

> And there was a man who came to him and asked, "Master, what good deed must I do to possess eternal life?" Jesus said to him, ". . .If you wish to enter into life, keep the commandments." He said, "Which?" "These:" Jesus replied "You must not kill. You must not commit adultery. You must not bring false witness. Honour your father

and mother, and: you must love your neighbor as yourself." The young man said to him, "I have kept all these. What more do I need to do?" Jesus said, "If you wish to be perfect, go and sell what you own and give the money to the poor, and you will have treasure in heaven; then come, follow me". But when the young man heard these words he went away sad, for he was a man of great wealth.

Then Jesus said to his disciples, "I tell you solemnly, it will be hard for a rich man to enter the kingdom of heaven. Yes, I tell you again, it is easier for a camel to pass through the eye of a needle than for a rich man to enter the kingdom of heaven." When the disciples heard this they were astonished. "Who can be saved, then?" they said. Jesus gazed at them. "For men" he told them "this is impossible; for God everything is possible."

Then Peter spoke. "What about us?" he said to him "We have left everything and followed you. What are we to have, then?" Jesus said to him, "I tell you solemnly, when it is all made new and the Son of Man sits on his throne of glory, you will yourselves sit on twelve thrones to judge the twelve tribes of Israel. And everyone who has left houses, brothers, sisters, father, mother, children or land for the sake of my name will be repaid a hundred times over, and also inherit eternal life" (Matthew 19, 16-29).

Jesus meets the conventional questions with what starts out to be a conventional response. How have eternal life? He lists several items in the Law. The man is pleased: he has done well by the Law. But then Jesus goes on. That is not sufficient, there is more to do. If he really wishes to lay hold of eternal life, then he must liquidate all his assets, abandon the proceeds to the poor, and follow Jesus on his wanderings.

Some interpreters have suggested that the passage offers a
double standard: a set of minimum requirements for everyday observants, who must keep the commandments, and a
higher way for those elite in the Church (monks, friars, nuns,
and the like) who are zestful enough to follow a more exact-
ing regime of self-denial. But the gospel cannot support such a
meaning. Jesus is presenting a single way of life, the only one
he urges as acceptable. The plight of his interlocutor is sad,
for his assets are many but his courage slight. He goes off in
the opposite direction. The point of the story is one of the
points of Matthew's gospel: the young man does not attain
eternal life, even though he has abided by the commandments. Keeping the Law does not nearly reach what Jesus
demands, nor does it reconcile one with the Father.

Jesus is contrasting the previous claims of Judaism with
his own. When a young man came of age he encountered the
Law. He was served notice of what the Lord demanded of
him. He knew what he was getting into; he ratified the covenant with his eyes open. If he undertook to follow Jesus,
however, he did quite the contrary. Jesus, whose expectations could not be contained or expressed in any code, invited men to follow a person, rather than a law. They were
obliged to undertake commitments whose concrete content
was unknown, to make promises whose measure could never
be taken, to ratify a covenant whose terms could not be
previously foreseen even with the most open of eyes. Much
of the comfort in the Law came from its precision: one could
know what God required. But Jesus insists that the divine
demand knows no limits. In founding a covenant of faith,
more than of obedience, he invites men to make their
response, not in terms of conditions accepted, but in terms of
the needs of the person to whom fidelity is pledged. And
since Jesus is concretely to be identified with all neighbors in
need, there is no end to the service required.

Jesus does not reject commandments; they lay out for
men the good they must do and the evil they must avoid. But
he rejects a morality that is *based* upon commandments and

limited to them, because a law ethic always deludes one into thinking that God's demands are contained by the law. The claims of Jesus' Father are not to be found in the Law. They burst the Law. Instead, Jesus proposes a person-ethic: a claim that is as large as the wants of the world.

In setting aside law as a metaphor too weak to convey his preaching, Jesus replaces it with a much more rigorous alternative. His ethic is limitless, open-ended. His claim is such as to devour a man's life, to allow him no rest. Of course, Matthew's story is not to be spoiled by thinking Jesus is speaking only of wealth. In the end he makes clear that all the supports a man clings to must be released: kin, house, and land. In a word: home. A man must not remain focused upon those who belong to him, who serve him back. He must be out on the move, like his Master prowling for the unfortunate brothers who have need of him. Like the Law, home represents a claim on him that is limited and controllable.

Jesus as (neither) Lawgiver (nor) Judge

Note that throughout the gospels Jesus encounters many specific queries. "Why is it that John's disciples and the disciples of the Pharisees fast, but your disciples do not?" "Look, why are they doing something on the Sabbath day that is forbidden?" "Why do the scribes say that Elijah has to come first?" "Is it against the law for a man to divorce his wife?" "Is it permissible to pay taxes to Caesar or not?" "Sir, who is my neighbor?" Jesus, unlike John (or Paul), is not in the habit of offering specific answers.[1] Nor does he respond with more abstract principles of general wisdom. Most often he responds with riddles or stories which suggest a larger vision that renders the original question petty and needless. He always has more to say than their queries call for; his answers are too large for their questions. He declines to be a lawmaker. He is

[1]See C. H. Dodd, *Gospel and Law* (Cambridge University Press, 1951), for a comparison of the different ethical approaches of the gospels and of Paul's epistles.

not calling men back to Moses; he is calling them forward to
a measure of devotion that Moses never demanded.

The extraordinary character of Jesus' ethic can also be
found in his long series of injunctions in the Sermon on the
Mount (Matthew 5, 20-48). His disciples must have a virtue
deeper than that of the scribes and the Pharisees, who abide
by the Law. They have learnt how it was said to their ances-
tors. . .But *he* says to them. . .The old ordinances fail by default. They seem to put curbs on obligation. There must be a
new integrity, a reckless generosity. The quality and measure
of service that Jesus calls for can only partially be summed
up in the Golden Rule, which so many writers use to suggest
a parity between the ethic of Jesus and other religions:
"Treat others as you would like them to treat you" (Luke
6, 31; Matthew 7, 12). It is better captured in that other
maxim: "Listen, Israel, the Lord our God is the one Lord,
and you must love the Lord your God with all your heart,
with all your soul, with all your mind and with all your
strength; you must love your neighbor as yourself" (Mark 12,
29-30). Best of all it is suggested in John's quotation: "Just
as I have loved you, you also must love one another" (13,34).
The New Commandment begins with no more specifics than
Jesus' own example, a suggestion of how far one might love.

Jesus, the new Moses, strikes a new sort of covenant
between the Lord and his people. He has but one command:
that men love one another as he has loved. He does not
oppose the Torah or reject it: he snubs it. He sweeps aside all
systems of law, which presume to define and thus to limit the
Father's claims and man's possibilities. Jesus charges each
man with full responsibility for his brothers and their needs,
and renders the analogy of law inadequate for the Christian
tradition. Thus he is no lawgiver, no legislator.[2]

[2]See the very incisive argument of C. F. D. Moule, "Important Moral
Issues—Prolegomena: The New Testament and Moral Decisions," *The Expository
Times*, LXXIV (1963/4), 370-73. Moule insists that the New Testament declines
to offer any specific moral directions, but instead refers the believer to the joint
and ongoing deliberations of the Christian worshipping congregation listening
critically.

Nor do the gospels care to call him judge. One story illustrating this is in the fifth chapter of John's gospel. Jesus heals a man who had for 38 years been a helpless paralytic. It is the sabbath, and certain onlookers challenge Jesus for leading the man to break the rest laws (by trying out his new walking legs, and carrying around his sleeping mat). Jesus meets the criticism by claiming exemption from this law. "His answer to them was, 'My Father goes on working, and so do I'. But that only made the Jews even more intent on killing him, because, not content with breaking the sabbath, he spoke of God as his own Father, and so made himself God's equal" (vss. 17-18).

His reply, at first somewhat mystifying, bears explanation. Despite the first chapter of Genesis, it was a contemporary theological belief that the Lord did not, in fact, cease all his activity on the sabbath. There were two prerogatives that he could not delegate to men: life-giving and judging. The rabbis noted that men were born indiscriminately on Saturday as well as on the other weekdays. Men died, too, without respect to the calendar. Each occasion—birth or death—required that he exercise one of these two sovereign powers, life-giving and judging. Thus the opinion that he was ceaselessly active. Jesus' claim to share the Father's seven-day work week implies that he also shared these exclusively divine powers. The implication was not lost on his audience, and he was accused of claiming equality with God.

John further implies that life-giving and judgment in the deeper sense do not occur at the two ends of a lifetime, at birth and at death, but at life's climax: encounter with the Lord. A man who for virtually a lifetime (40 years was the round number for a generation) had been as good as dead meets Jesus. He is given life — not simply the ability to walk, but what that was meant to stand for: the strength to walk in God's paths, to stay clear of sin. There was an immediate reaction among the bystanders, this way and that. Some said it was God's work, others fell to grumbling about the sabbath rules. According to John, Jesus simply confronts the crowd

with an act of raw benevolence, and their reactions to him
reveal their own hearts. Some cherish the itinerant healer for
doing a favor, others revile him. There is no quarrel over
whether or not he is divine, but simply whether he is a good
or a lawless man. Unwittingly, by taking sides when the
divine benevolence is exposed to them, they judge themselves. Some come away with life, and some display their
death. The unleashing of God's graciousness in human affairs
makes it unnecessary to wait until death for men to be
divided: the judgment event is in the ever contemporaneous
Now.

John inverts the traditional sense of judgment. The
radical sense of the New Testament word for judging,
κρίνειν, is "to cleave, to divide". Jesus can claim, "I judge
no one" (8, 15), for it is not he who scrutinizes a man's life
and declares where he stands. He enters a village and gives
heart and life to someone in need. By the time he leaves,
everyone has taken sides. What this reveals is not simply what
kind of person *he* is, but what kind *they* are, how they stand
with regard to benevolence, to grace, to the Father. The
encounter with goodness provokes men to judge themselves.

> Thus, as the Father raises the dead and gives them life,
> so the Son gives life to anyone he chooses;
> for the Father judges no one;
> so that all may honour the Son
> as they honour the Father.
> Whoever refuses honour to the Son
> refuses honour to the Father who sent him.
> I tell you most solemnly,
> whoever listens to my words
> and believes in the one who sent me,
> has eternal life;
> without being brought to judgement
> he has passed from death to life.
> I tell you most solemnly,

the hour will come—in fact it is here already—
when the dead will hear the voice of the Son of God,
and all who hear it will live.
For the Father, who is the source of life,
has made the Son the source of life;
and, because he is the Son of Man,
has appointed him supreme judge. (5, 21-27)

The gospels do identify Jesus as lawgiver and as judge, but go to great pains to show that these analogies are transfigured far above their conventional meaning. I am inclined to doubt whether Christian moral theology has continued to notice the startling innovation which Jesus was evidently at such pains to offer. For the old themes of legislation and judgment are usually worked into our preaching in ways that would make Moses happier than they would Jesus.

Two Stories of Salvation

The rudimentary structure beneath almost all Christian moralizing is what I suggest calling the "forensic metaphor". Like the savior myth, it is nowhere set down in simple and brief fashion, but let me try to sketch it out.

Men live under the legitimate authority of God, whose sovereign rights as creator are limitless. God has established a law, a code of commandments for men, which he makes known in various ways. First, there is the subtle, stirring voice of right-and-wrong in every man's conscience (often called the natural law). Then there are the laws of Moses revealed to Israel, and the more explicit revelation through Jesus to the Christian Church. Although God's statutes bind all men, they are not evenly known from man to man. All, however, are expected to have a grasp of at least the basic obligations. Thus warned, each man has a lifetime of freedom to behave as he will, but at the end he will be judged on how well he has kept the law. God will then call him to account for everything he has done, though taking into consideration all the extenuating circumstances which might modify guilt: ignorance of the law, a strong impulse or passion that may have swept him into evil without his really choosing it, lack of foresight about the harm he was causing others, etc. After all this is reckoned up, a final verdict is issued, and the man is consigned appropriately to either eternal reward or eternal punishment.

The forensic metaphor, even in briefest form, suggests how the commonly-held folk-ethic of Christians is at odds with the Jesus-ethic in the gospel. In imitation of the civil law, God is seen as both legislator and as judge. He gives the laws to begin with, and at the end holds men responsible for having observed them. His legal demands, even if numerous, are limited. There is little hint of the gospel call to give one's whole heart, to unleash one's full strength, to follow Jesus in search of all man's sufferings and want. Nor is there any room for the changeless benevolence of Jesus' Father, who loves without restraint.

When ethics are cast into the mould of law (rather than incorporating law as an appendage to some other ethical metaphor), sin is portrayed, not as an intrinsic disorder and disaster within the person, but as a disobedient rejection of authority, disastrous only because recorded and punished.[3] Virtue is no matter of growth with the person, but of conformity whose reward is given by an observant God. It is not of itself reward enough. Since sin is a purposeful defiance

---

[3]It is interesting in this regard to study *The Common Law* by Oliver Wendell Holmes, ed. Mark DeWolfe Howe (Cambridge: Belknap, 1963). His thesis is that the tendency of law is to move away from moral standards and to seek external ones. Less and less it considers malice, guilt, or moral conscience, requiring external conformity to standards of conduct, and replacing estimates of moral intention with legal presumptions from empirical behavior.

of the divine will, revelation of the law is hardly an advantage, a grace. If anything, it is a burden, for ignorance of the law could be an excuse to behave according to one's own whim. In a word, the forensic metaphor undergirds an ethic that is extrinsic. The law is an advertisement, not of what corrupts man or makes him grow, but of what God forbids or imposes.

Admittedly every metaphor must be allowed to limp a little, but I am arguing that this one, so familiar to popular Christian teaching, denies the very points that the gospel is at pains to emphasize. In its place I would venture to offer what might be called the "confrontation metaphor."

Every man has his life to live. During that brief, critical time he must grow. Beginning as a totally self-centered infant, he must be transformed into one who is totally given to others in generous love. He interacts with his fellows, immensely affected by them, yet picking his own way along the path that offers many turning points. He may know what kind of God cares for him, what sort of person he is himself becoming. But also, he may know none of these things. If he does, so much the better. What is essential, however, is that he grow to fullest human stature, that he become a man who loves heartily. At death time will end, growth will cease. What he has become, that he will remain forever. At death he confronts God. If he is a man who has grown into love, he will draw near and cleave to him—as he has gone out of himself to his brothers before death. If he has only become wrapped up in himself, then he will come face-to-face with the Lord, but not notice him any more than he has noticed his brothers. Death is now the occasion for fullest revelation more than for reward or punishment: yet only those with eyes to see will see.

According to this model, God does not alter his attitudes with human behavior: his is an unyielding welcome. Since good and evil, growth and corruption, are values in themselves, ethics are a matter of what man is, rather than what he intends. But revelation is a gift, for it discloses to man what it is to his advantage to know. In the forensic metaphor, virtue and sin are oddly symmetrical: both are possessed only insofar as a man is consciously and purposefully acting. If anything, the conscience of the sinner is portrayed as the more active, the more agitated. In the confrontation metaphor, on the contrary, sin is not seen as the conscious choice of evil so much as the subtle and obstinate avoidance of neighbor need, the self-inflicted anaesthesia of conscience. Sin involves the smothering of responsibility; it is not defiance, but neglect. In the end a man is not judged for what he has responsibly done right or wrong. He is simply presented to God as he is, and he relates to him accordingly.

Perhaps the point can be illustrated by several anecdotes. The first is provided by Jesus himself in Luke 16, 19-31. There was a man who dressed well, ate well, and went to hell. No crime is held against him; there is no accusation of debauchery. But during all those years there had been a man at his door who did not eat well (in fact, he had only the scraps from the man's kitchen), and who had only his own sores as wearing apparel (one thinks of the kwashiorkor that comes with famine). During all those years the rich man had come and gone upon his business, never noticing Lazarus. The great gulf that he beheld between himself and Lazarus, who went to be comforted in the company of Abraham, had been fixed long before he ever died. And Abraham told him that if his five brothers were as blind as he to other men, then surely no messenger from the dead would be able to break through to them. They see what they wish to see. This reinforces Jesus' claim elsewhere that those who cannot hear what he is saying or see what he is doing have closed themselves off to all brothers, not just to him or to the Father. Note that men are lost without any hint of divine wrath. The love of God is not sentimental: it pours forth lavishly to men, but unless they open to it, they will surely be destroyed. In the end, it will be in vain that God has loved a man, if that man not become one who loves.

Another suggestive text is found in *The Towers of Trebizond,* an otherwise bizarre travel book by the late Rose Macaulay. The scene in question finds her poking through the ruins of a Byzantine church in Trebizond:

> It took me some time to make out the Greek inscription, which was about saving me from my sins, and I hesitated to say this prayer, as I did not really want to be saved from my sins, not for the time being, it would make things too difficult and too sad [she was at the time having an affair with someone else's husband]. I was getting into a stage when I was not quite sure what sin was, I was in a kind of fog, drifting about without clues, and this is liable to happen when you go on and on doing something, it makes a confused sort of twilight in which everything is blurred, and the next thing you know you might be stealing or anything, because right and wrong have become things you do not look at, you are afraid to, and it seems better to live in a blur. Then come the times when you wake suddenly up, and the fog breaks, and right and wrong loom through it, sharp and clear like peaks of rock, and you are on the wrong peak and know that, unless you can manage to leave it now, you may be marooned there for life and ever after. Then, as you don't leave it, the mist swirls round again, and hides the other peak, and you turn your back on it and try to forget it and succeed.
>
> Another thing you learn about sin, it is not one deed more than another, though the Church may call some of them mortal and others not, but even the worst ones are only. . .a chain, not things by themselves, and adultery, say, is chained with

stealing sweets when you are a child, or taking
another child's toys, or the largest piece of cake, or
letting someone else be thought to have broken
something you have broken yourself, or breaking
promises and telling secrets, it is all one thing and
you are tied up with that chain till you break it,
and the Church calls it not being in a state of
grace.[4]

The third anecdote is from an adaptation of Pinnocchio.
The hero of the story is a very self-centered, young puppet.
To cure him of his egotism, he was given an increasingly long
nose, but it seems that even this disfigurement failed to evoke
the desired repentance. More draconian measures were
needed. Pinnocchio was therefore taken on a guided tour of
hell, in hopes that the sights there might shock him into
virtue. The first person he encountered in the underworld
was a lady ballet dancer. She was dancing with great
concentration when he approached to interview her. He
found that she danced right past him, and no amount of
effort succeeded in catching her attention. Moving along, he
came upon a carpenter hard at work: sawing, fitting, and
gluing his woodwork. He, too, proved impossible to inter-
rupt, no matter how insistently the little puppet-man tried to
catch his eye. It was at this point that Pinnocchio saw, in a
flash, that in hell everyone is left to himself, to do only what
he wants to do and to take no notice of anyone else. And,
now that he remembered, people were like this already on
earth. He returned to the upper world a repentant puppet.

In proposing that the Christian ethic should not be
modelled around the metaphor of law, I am trying to
highlight the more stringent and more internal ethic implied
in the gospel. Classical theology has maintained that one
could sin only if he were aware of it. This flies in the face of

---

[4](New York: Farrar, Straus and Cudahy, 1956), p. 150.

common observation. We do not notice — we do not allow ourselves to notice — human need that we are unwilling to relieve. Sin brings the hardened heart, the deafened ear, the unseeing eye, the limp conscience: the very contrary of awareness. Active love, like that of Jesus, is most sensitive, and discovers without being told who is suffering, who lies neglected.

It is precisely the man who lies helpless in his own blindness that needs revelation. For ignorance of oneself is not bliss. He has need of his neighbor to pierce through his smokescreen and disclose to him that he is wretchedly and pitiably poor, and blind and naked too. If the rebuke comes as part of the authentic Christian revelation, it brings two advantages. First, the man discovers that his selfishness and estrangement are of eternal importance. Second, in the forgiveness of the Father, embodied in the humble and humane bluntness of his brother, he finds the support that it takes to see himself as he really is. Revelation in time is a grace, for it opens eyes to see the blinding welcome that lies beyond time.

Situation Ethics

What I am offering as a renewed ethical approach may seem at first sight to resemble another system of thought that has attracted much attention today: situation ethics. I view situation ethics as a very flawed representation of Christian morality. Nevertheless, both because it has drawn to its service some of the more capable penmen in theology, and because it provides a good foil for the thesis I am putting forward, I should like to offer an extended critique of situation ethics.[5] The handiest way is to review *Situation*

[5]Most of what follows is adapted from an article, "The Conservatism of Situation Ethics, "published in *New Blackfriars*, October, 1966, pp. 7-14, and used here by kind permission of the editor.

Ethics, the work of Joseph Fletcher, for many years professor of social ethics at the Episcopal Theological Seminary in Cambridge, Massachusetts.[6] He has been active in ethical debate since the days when the Old Morality was the Newest thing around, and his espousal of situationism is clear and attractive.

Dr. Fletcher, if I understand him correctly, repudiates the Old Morality because it is legalistic. It takes the form of a code, a list of commandments which assign an invariable moral value to certain acts. The circumstances attending these acts may, it is granted, slightly modify their morality. But the ultimate and overriding source of good and evil is the very nature of the acts. Against such a view Fletcher urges that no action is good or evil in itself. It cannot be judged in isolation from its meaningful and meaning-giving context of circumstances. The morality of any action is correlative to the love it expresses. Admittedly there are many deeds which are usually sinful (e.g., abortion, lying, arson, extramarital intercourse). This is not because they are intrinsically evil acts, but because they most often embody selfishness, exploitation of one's neighbour, and irresponsibility. In certain extraordinary circumstances these actions might so bespeak commitment and caring and sincerity that, viewed in their contextual totality, they would be adjudged good and virtuous. Since morality is not intrinsic to acts, we can never resort to inflexible ethical laws or norms. At best we can employ maxims, from which we must always be prepared, in some situations, to deviate.

We are offered, says New Moralist Fletcher, only three ethical approaches. There is legalism, which lays down a code of predetermined norms, commandments that establish invariably which acts are good and which evil. Catholics have tended to derive their laws from reason, while Protestants

[6](Philadelphia: Westminster, 1966).

customarily extract theirs from the Bible. But there is little difference: both pharisaically reduce Christian ethics to a manual of absolute rules for mechanical consultation. Secondly, there is antinomianism, which reckons every human event to be so singular and incomparable that no principles could possibly have universal validity. One must wait until the moment of decision, and trust to the guidance of the Spirit to inspire a spontaneous moral judgment "on the spot." Situationism is deftly presented as an alternative to these two extremes. "The situationist enters into every decision-making situation fully armed with the ethical maxims of his community and its heritage, and he treats them with respect as illuminators of his problems. Just the same he is prepared in any situation to compromise them or set them aside *in the situation* if love seems better served by doing so" (p.26). Fletcher will neither be bound by norms nor discard them entirely. He accepts them, but only as cautious generalizations, working rules that are expected to break down in extraordinary circumstances. He "keeps principles sternly in their place, in the role of advisers without veto power!" (p.55).

Natural law ethics has customarily claimed to deduce its first principles from a study of man and society. Dr. Fletcher states that the first principle of situation ethics cannot be deduced, validated, or even discussed. There is no metaphysic that can lead the mind up to faith, by proving that God exists. Likewise there is no reasonable argument that can prove that man ought to love. It is the irrational, arbitrary leap of faith that posits love as the *summum bonum.* Christian morality sets out from a decision, not from a deduction. "Any moral or value judgment in ethics, like a theologian's faith proposition, is a *decision*—not a conclusion. It is a choice, not a result reached by force of logic, Q.E.D. The hedonist cannot 'prove' that pleasure is the highest good, any more than the Christian can 'prove' that love is!" (p.47).

Situation ethics, the author tells us, is no system, no

computerized conscience with answers to moral dilemmas. He nevertheless consents to formulate the insights of his method in six propositions:

1. *Only one "thing" is intrinsically good; namely, love: nothing else at all.*
Fletcher sides firmly with the nominalists, who say that goodness is only a predicate, never a property. Nothing possesses moral value by itself; it can only be assigned value by reference to persons. "Hence it follows that in Christian situation ethics nothing is worth anything in and of itself. It gains or acquires its value only because it happens to help persons (thus being good) or to hurt persons (thus being bad)" (p. 59). Goodness, then, is nothing intrinsic or objective; it flows solely from the loving purpose with which one acts for the benefit of other persons.

2. *The ruling norm of Christian decision is love: nothing else.*
Immature Christians would always rather escape the burdens of responsibility. Law ethics has been a comfort to such folk, because it replaces freedom with security. There are no dilemmas to be faced, only statutes to be consulted. The situationist, rejecting the plea of Dostoevsky's Grand Inquisitor, claims that there is only one absolute obligation: love. All other laws will sooner or later conflict with love, and are therefore only relative, unauthoritative, voidable.

3. *Love and justice are the same, for justice is love distributed, nothing else.*
Fletcher deplores the traditional theological distinction between justice and love (justice gives a person his due, is obligatory; love gives him beyond his due, is optional). Real love, he says, seeks the greatest good for the greatest number of persons. It is calculating, prudent, shrewd, and efficient; it uses its head, it figures all the angles. What might at first sight

seem to be loving behavior to one's immediate neighbor could, on a broader social calculus, show up as hurtful to the common weal. Conversely, treatment of individuals usually considered immoral may be justified by the benefits it brings to the community.

4.   Love wills the neighbour's good whether we like him or not.

With Bultmann he states, "In reality, the love which is based on emotions of sympathy, or affection, is self-love; for it is a love of preference, of choice, and the standard of the preference and choice is the self" (p. 104). Love is not liking, not a feeling of benevolence. Feeling, in fact, is not capable of being commanded as love is. Love is impartial in that it focuses its concern, not on those neighbours who are liked, but on those neighbours who are more numerous or more in need.

5.   Only the end justifies the means; nothing else.

Means are neutral tools, with no moral content but what the end gives to them. Fletcher insists he is not advocating the choice of evil means to a good end; any means to a good end becomes, by that fact, good. He gives the example of two episodes in the American pioneer West, when parties of settlers were being pursued by Indians. "(1) A Scottish woman saw that her suckling baby, ill and crying, was betraying her and her three other children, and the whole company, to the Indians. But she clung to her child, and they were caught and killed. (2) A Negro woman, seeing how her crying baby endangered another trail party, killed it with her own hands, to keep silence and reach the fort" (pp. 124-25). Fletcher infers that the second woman made the right situationist decision. Taking one innocent life was good because by it many innocent lives were saved. The only self-validating end for a Christian is love; all means and subordinate ends must be justified by reference to that.

*6.   Love's   decisions   are   made   situationally,   not
prescriptively.*

Since it is impossible to know in advance, in ignorance
of the situation and consequences of an act, whether it is
loving or not, one must await the moment itself and make
the ethical judgment then, not by consulting a prefab set of
rules.

It is disappointing that Professor Fletcher's book,
intended mainly as a critique of the Old Morality, has not
located very accurately his real grievance with the traditional
system. Ethics, especially Catholic ethics, has been much
more situational than he seems to notice. It is very difficult,
perhaps impossible, to find a single act which of its intrinsic
nature, stripped of all circumstances, was presented as
absolutely immoral. The old moralists used to say that
blasphemy was the only intrinsically evil act they could think
of—but, like suicide, it is difficult to imagine it as a sane act.
In fact, the prohibitions of the Old Morality have all been
highly situational; the very definitions of lying, killing,
stealing, etc., include situational factors. Lying is evil, they
said, but lying is described situationally: telling a direct
falsehood to someone who has a right to the truth, except in
jocularity, etc. Killing is evil (unless it is the only means of
self-defense against murderous assault, or the only effective
means of sanction to protect a community from serious
criminal harm, etc., etc.) Stealing is evil (unless to redress
injustice, or when one's need is urgent enough to nullify
another's claim to superfluous property, or the public good
requires confiscation or nationalization, etc., etc.).

The Old Morality never said that the situation was
ethically negligible. On the contrary, it simply asserted that
once certain combinations of disqualifying circumstances are
present, no additional circumstances can redeem that default.
Once it is established that the woman with whom a man
performs the symbolic sexual celebration of total, unconditioned commitment is not in fact the person to whom he is

so committed (i.e., his wife), then the act is seen to be evil, no matter what other situational variables you may care to add. And once it is established that the person whom a man slays is entirely innocent (e.g., an unborn child), the situation renders the act evil. Both Old and New Moralists are situational; but the one denies and the other affirms that a fundamental evil in the situation can be outweighed by other, good circumstances.

What Fletcher and others want is a set of maxims of general but not invariable validity, a system of guidelines with allowances for extraordinary situations that could justify otherwise sinful acts. On the level of popular morality this would, of course, conflict with the notion of commandments. But the real disagreement is even deeper. The Old Morality has held it as axiomatic that any human action involves four distinguishable ethical factors: (1) the motive of the agent; (2) the intrinsic nature of the act; (3) its foreseen effects; (4) the modifying circumstances. For an action to be morally good, all four factors must be good; for it to be evil, it suffices that a single factor be evil. Thus the theorem: *Bonum ex integra causa; malum de quocumque defectu.* (The fixation of Catholic moralists on sin is due, not simply to the fact that they wrote manuals for confessors, but also to the divergent attitudes of this theorem to good and evil. Determine that an action is good, and you say only that it *may* be done; numerous other good options are available. Establish that it is evil, and you say that it *must not* be done. In dietetics they say that fruits, cheeses, meats, wines, cereals, and milk are all possible features of a balanced diet, but no single item is a must. On the other hand, it can be said definitely that prussic acid is a must not. So with the soul, pathology is more definite than physiology; imperatives are attached more easily to evil than to good acts.) The Old Morality has held that goodness is indivisible: for an act to be good each separate factor must be good. The New Morality seems to contend that goodness is divisible: the evil of one factor may be cancelled out by the prevailing good of the others.

Morals are the Making of Man

Despite its name, situation ethics does not revolve on situation at all. Fletcher moves about—messily at times, it seems—from motive to consequences to situation. But the crucial factor in the method is motive. The system really should be called intention ethics. What is novel about it is the claim that any action, in any situation, with any consequences, is good if it is an action of love, and evil if an action of nonlove. Love, urges Fletcher, is the only norm, the only measure. All ethical judgment must therefore revolve about purpose. It is essentially indifferent what forms a man's behavior takes, provided this behavior be the outward expression of inward caring. No one can ever be blamed if his intentions were good. In other words, the moral value of a man's deeds is wholly contained in the purpose he brings to them. It is precisely this axiom which I feel to be both the pivot and the weakness of the entire system. The New Moralists are saying that the moral value of an act is what you put into it. They neglect, it seems to me, that it also involves what you get out of the act.

On a phenomenological view, human behavior consists of countless day-to-day actions scattered across the surface of our lives. Generally we put very little of ourselves into any particular act. We do not manifest our full and true person in any one moment. If we should be voluntarily crucified or something like that, we would most likely be drawing ourselves up to full strength, so to speak—but we are not often voluntarily crucified. Single actions are not expressive of our total character nor utterly decisive in our life. But over a period of time certain characteristic trends and traits appear, personality patterns emerge, an overall direction of our affairs is felt and observed. In a certain sense it is right to speak of a duality here—not a severance between intention and deed, but a dialectic between this fundamental option (let us say, our fundamental selfishness or selflessness) and the complex of individual actions. What I do and what I am are constantly interacting upon one another. My character discloses itself in what I do, yet can be shaped and modified by changes in what I do. My life works from the inside out and *also* from the outside in. In Christian terms, the state of grace and the state of sin refer to this deep level of fundamental option which is forming and stabilizing itself over the course of a lifetime. It would be difficult to localize conversion or serious sin within any singular act, and unobservant to assert that there could be much short-term oscillation between one fundamental option and its opposite. Yet these states are slowly entered and reinforced by the swarm of minor daily deeds. Fletcher, it appears, acknowledges only a one-way traffic: he points out—quite well—how purpose shapes deeds, but neglects that conversely deeds shape purpose.

This is illustrated by a case he presents elsewhere:

How are we to "judge" the Puerto Rican woman in Bruce Kendrick's story about the East Harlem Protestant Parish, *Come out the Wilderness.* She was proud of her son and told the minister how she had "made friends" with a married man, praying God she'd have a son, and eventually she bore one. The minister, dear silly man that he is, told her it was okay if she was repentant, and she replied, "Repent? I ain't repentin. I asked the Lord for my boy. He's a gift from God." She is *right* (which, by the way, does *not* mean a situationist approves in the abstract of the absence of any husband in so many disadvantaged Negro and Puerto Rican families).[7]

[7]*Commonweal*, January 14, 1966, p. 428.

Herbert McCabe retorts in the same issue:

> No, not in the abstract, just in the concrete. "She
> is right" is a betrayal of the revolution that is
> required in East Harlem. Of course such a woman
> caught up and lost in the jungle of the acquisitive
> society may be blameless, may be a saint, and of
> course the first thing that matters is to understand
> and sympathize with her immediate position; but
> she is *wrong*. To say she is right is to accept, as she
> does, the social situation in which she lives. A
> genuine moral judgment cuts deeper than that; it
> questions such a "situation" in terms of something
> greater. When we say "you can't apply the same
> high moral standards to slaves as you do to us" we
> accept slavery as an institution. Of course to
> punish or condemn the slave for lying or stealing is
> to hit the wrong target; it is the masters who bear
> the blame, but the blame is for the slave's wrong
> action.[8]

Here we have a paradigm of the various moralities. The
minister, representing the Old Morality, says the woman has
acted wrongly, and is guilty. Fletcher says that her motives
were good; in light of the local situation she has acted rightly,
and is not guilty. McCabe says that in light of the total
situation she has acted wrongly, but is not guilty (the guilt
accrues to Harlem's makers). But all three positions are
caught up in a superficial praise-and-blame morality. Fletcher
does not adequately suggest that often the Christian's duty is
not to conform to the situation but to repudiate it, even to
refashion it. And even McCabe cannot be urgently committed
to a revolution in East Harlem, if it is likely that "such a
woman, caught up and lost in the jungle of the acquisitive
society may be blameless, may be a saint." The terrible thing
about Harlem is that it smothers the integrity of its people, it

[8]*Ibid.*, p. 440.

makes them evil people. Harlem's makers are not those who kill the body, but cannot kill the soul. They are those who are able to destroy both body and soul in hell, and this is why Harlem is hell. It is never radical enough to admit that an evil situation has made the poor woman act wrongly, while leaving her blameless—it has wreaked a far more tragic evil upon her, it has made her absorb its evil values. (The same, of course, might be said of Grosse Point or San Sebastian or Rome.)

The myopia in a praise-and-blame ethics is that it ignores the dialectic between singular acts and overall orientation, deed and intention. A morality that is concerned with guilt or innocence thinks of acts only as responsible expressions of the self, and neglects that they are also shapers of the self. Now the fact that repetitive evil actions incur guilt is extrinsic; the intrinsic, and to my mind more important, fact is that they make the doer less loving. A young boy who grows up in Harlem may, through no fault of his own, take his recreation by slashing automobile tires, robbing drunks, petty thieving, and taking heroin. It is absurd to suggest that, since there is no malevolence involved and he is the creature of his situation, he is doing right. It is irrelevant to say he is doing wrong, but that the guilt falls upon others. The tragedy is that morally he has been destroyed by a course of actions which he may have entered with no particular evil intent. A young girl who knows no better may take to bed with her a new boyfriend every week, simply because this is the accepted way of showing affection and holding a partner in her milieu. It is simply not meaningful to call her guilty or guiltless. What can be said is that she has corroded through unwitting misuse her own capacity to love. A Pennsylvania mine owner in the last century may have taken it for granted that young women and children were effective workers if put to crawling through tunnels, dragging loads of coal. He probably did not choose overtly to exploit them, yet gradually and imperceptibly the

situation was likely to make him exploitative, and to kill his
sensitivity and respect for persons. A child brought up in an
unstable home has harm done to his loving-power that is not
of his own choosing. Sin, it seems to me, has too often been
imagined as a responsible decision to do evil. What I see of it
seems rather to be a suffocation of responsibility through
repetitive actions which generally avoid any open decision.
We have made "good" into a legal metaphor corresponding to
"responsibility" and "guilt"; in a world where there is all too
little responsibility but much evil, it seems not the most
helpful metaphor to employ in theology, Old or New.
Remember that in Christ's parable on judgment the condemned are sent away for offences that were unwitting; by
doing unloving things they had become unloving, to their
surprise.

Consequently my distress for the East Harlem woman is
that with the best intentions, with the worst situation, she
has done something which has hurt her. And my distress with
the New Morality is that it is shallow and legalistic. It ignores
that there are false, selfish, and evil actions which, regardless
of our motives for performing them, can corrupt our ability
to love, and that moral value is somehow objective as well as
subjective. Situational variables may anaesthetize us to moral
pain or mitigate the damage, but damage there is. We cannot
long go through the motions of lovelessness without one day
waking up to discover we have killed our love. Like Pontius
Pilate.

One of the great weaknesses of the Old Morality is its
refusal to allow for extraordinary exceptions in its absolute
laws. Indeed, *the* weakness is in using the notion of law at all.
The New Morality's criticism of this weakness is disappointing because it is so half-hearted and conservative. It shares the
Old idea that morality has to do with guilt or innocence, with
responsibility. It thus ignores that much of the evil we do is
not due to our evil intentions and purposes, but to the evil
values that our cultural milieu foists upon us. A situation

ethic should recognize more clearly that our situation is to a large degree evil, and that our worry should be to defend ourselves against the false values accepted in our society. Ethics cannot afford to be individualistic, when so much of the lovelessness in individuals is inherited from a bad society. The Christian's duty is so often to fight free of his situation, though he may apparently be destroyed in the process. Like Christ.

Philemon's problem, imposed upon him by this Christ, is that the memory of crucifixion and the vision of resurrection summon him beyond his plans, desires, and struggles to be a virtuous man. There is no longer any question of what he could settle for. His plans are dissolved; his desires, rendered puny; his struggles, not so fatiguing. Instead of reaching for those good actions he must or may perform, he is drawn after possibilities of love that stretch endlessly on. Situation ethics, as also that tepid ethical system it wishes to supplant, shrinks back from this very surrender of self which Christian faith is all about. It seeks to foreclose alternatives, whereas an authentic moral drive opens up more and more alternatives: not what might be more excusable, but what might be more creative or generous or honorable. The best hope for Philemon is that he be somehow enabled to see beyond his situation to an ethic of a better day.

4 An Ethic Both Personal and Social

For one who believes that the Father of Jesus loves and draws to himself all men without regard for their behavior, conventional Christian ethics must undergo profound re-arrangement. It is ever crucial for man to discern good and evil, and to act accordingly. However, the purpose for which he must so govern himself is not to secure God's welcome, which is assured him in any case. It is rather that he might grow and mature into love, lest infinite cherishing be lost upon him, and he be disabled from responding to that welcome.

The moral charge of Jesus of Nazareth, peculiar among this world's ethics, is no program for minimal integrity, but an outright demand that men abandon themselves to limitless generosity. Thus, although the Church may, has, and does frame commandments, they are not divine laws, but human advice about how to respond to the divine call. Their publication as if from God is a literary and homiletic custom, bespeaking the unchanged conviction that all moral behavior is no simple matter between man and men, but creative of bonds with the Lord.

I have had some words of criticism for preachers and theologians who present Christian morality in unrelieved terms of reward or punishment, praise or blame for responsible deeds. Thereby they obscure the dissimilarity between virtue and sin, which respectively enhance and destroy responsibility. They also obscure the intrinsic and immediate outcome of good or evil actions, in favor of some final resolution at the time of death. In a word, although we are creatures, the Lord who loves us without measure offers the overwhelming invitation to respond with measureless love. It has often been the desire of moral theologians to persuade believers that Jesus had more modest and more petty plans.

In this chapter I should like to explore the paradoxes and confusions that darken the relationship between personal ethics and social ethics. I have been making the case that the ethical enterprise of man in the care of his all-cherishing Lord is a venture towards fullest personal growth and at the same time a commitment to the needs of neighbors. It rises from within a single man's conscience, yet is beholden to the collective wisdom of the family of man. In purpose and in source, ethics has to be both individual and social, though in diverse ways. Oversimplified theories of morality have tended to yield to one or another of these, and let the other go. The pages that follow will ponder several inescapable features, individual and social, that must be accounted for in any full moral system.

Decisions: The Core of Ethics

One very personal feature of morals that deserves heightened emphasis is the need for *choice*. The call from Jesus to wholehearted service confronts every believer with the vast claims of human want. Yet he is so limited in time, wit, and wealth. He will grow, and his capacities will stretch. But even with appetite and performance enlarging, choices have to be made.

One of the stories that best conveys this is in Matthew's Gospel:

> When the Son of Man comes in his glory, escorted by all the angels, he will take his seat on his throne of glory. All the nations will be assembled before him and he will separate men one from another as the shepherd separates sheep from goats. He will place the sheep on his right hand and the goats on his left. Then the King will say to those on his right hand, "Come, you whom my Father has blessed, take for your heritage the kingdom prepared for you since the foundation of the world. For I was hungry and you gave me food; I was thirsty and you gave me drink; I was a stranger and you made me welcome; naked and you clothed me, sick and you visited me, in prison and you came to see me." Then the virtuous will say to him in reply, "Lord, when did we see the hungry and feed you; or thirsty and give you drink? When did we see you a stranger and make you welcome; naked and clothe you; sick or in prison and go to see you?" And the King will answer, "I tell you solemnly, in so far as you did this to one of the least of these brothers of mine, you did it to me". Next he will say to those on his left hand, "Go away from me, with your curse upon you, to the eternal fire prepared for the devil and his angels. For I was hungry, and you never gave me food; I was thirsty and you never gave me anything to drink; I was a stranger and you never made me welcome, naked and you never clothed me, sick and in prison and you never visited me." Then it will be their turn to ask, "Lord when did we see you hungry or thirsty, a stranger or naked, sick or in prison, and did not come to your help?" Then he will answer, "I tell you solemnly, in so far

as you neglected to do this to one of the least of
these, you neglected to do it to me". And they will
go away to eternal punishment, and the virtuous to
eternal life. (25, 31-46)

The format of the story follows classic Old Testament
lines: the Lord will judge, and mete out blessing for
obedience, curse for failure to obey. What is novel in Jesus'
version, though, is that there is no mention of the Law.
Those who are dismissed under curse are accused of no
violation of the commandments; in fact, to judge by their
surprise, they might have expected to survive judgment fairly
well in terms of the commandments. But the ground had
shifted under their feet. What they are condemned for is not
defiance of the Law, but failure to address themselves to the
miserable of the world. As pointed out in the preceding
chapter, this obligation, unlike those in the Law, is limitless.
It is possible for one to plead that he has supported his
elderly parents, resisted adultery, and stayed free of perjury.
But who is to say that he has fed the hungry, housed the
homeless, or aided the imprisoned? This obligation is as vast
as the numbers of hungry, homeless, and jailed. Further,
those who find themselves cursed are not rejected for what
they have done, but for what they have failed to do. Even
more, they are taken by surprise: they are guilty, not just for
what they failed to do, but for what it never *occurred* to
them to do.

The parable is disconcerting. God's claim, previously
manageable and measurable, is now as unfathomable as the
ills of mankind. For the Christian there is neither measure
nor limit offered for his observance. Yet his own capacities
seem so very measured and limited. Quite clearly, the good to
be done is not optional, yet it is described in infinite terms.
He is sent, not simply to keep himself clear of the world, but
to break into people's lives, to busy himself with their needs.
The good is commanded, not commended. One is burdened

with all human burdens, and there is no one to tell him just how far his own concrete contribution need go.

Curiously enough, the Christian community will offer faint counsel or help in this dilemma. The tradition will warn him away from perjury and incest and embezzlement. But it will not tell him or even suggest to him what career he should follow, what prices he should charge, what woman he should marry. Consider once more the asymmetry between good and evil to which the last chapter alluded. Moral counsel lends itself to imperatives more easily in negative than in positive matters, wherein one can rarely do more than indicate options. Misfortune gashes memory (both individual and collective) and enables a tradition to give explicit caveats against ill and degenerative behavior. The lamentable consequence is that the rest of human life — involving most positive decisions — has not been considered morally sensitive or significant. Most folk rarely feel under pressure to make moral decisions, since morality is understood only to forbid those sorts of crime and debauchery they are not bothered by anyhow.

In other words, we have come to think that where there are options, where there is freedom, our choices are ethically indifferent. The very opposite is true. It is mostly our free choices that are the making or the unmaking of us: our education, our careers, our marriages, the rearing of our children, political loyalties, toil and friendships. And here, too, we must be guided by imperatives. The gospel construes it so. Our lives must be turned to service. We stand in jeopardy if we fail to feed, house, clothe, heal, befriend, and defend our helpless brothers. Yet which brothers?

Here it is that we must turn option into imperative. There is no one who tells a man he *must* have three more children, or that he *must* support a certain candidate for mayor. No one can *command* a woman to take in her neighbor's children while on vacation, or tell her it is her *duty* to return to nursing after her children are out of infancy. For the nature of a positive imperative is somewhat different from a negative one. For negatives, a man can and should rely heavily upon the experience and the wisdom of the tradition, which advises him, "You must not. . ." For positives, more far-reaching and important, he must himself be creative, and decide for himself, not "I must," but "I shall". Self-determination is every bit as decisive, even though it begins from options.

Tom Dooley, for instance, decided to give his life to medical service in the frontier areas of Laos. He was free, yet he imposed it upon himself. The whole shape of his career was surely the largest moral issue in his life, and it grew from a commandment he imposed upon himself.

Even negative decisions are haunted by the need for personal choice. Thomas More decided at a certain point that he could no longer follow his king. Why at that particular point? As chancellor of England he had been the king's minister in more than one transaction that would have troubled a conscience as sensitive as his. On the other hand, it is conceivable that his fine and subtle purchase on the law could have permitted him to tolerate this matter of the king's annulment, only to find some other intolerable issue some years later. Yet why was it precisely at *this* point that More chose to dig in his heels, to opt out of the king's service? Another man of equal integrity might have said, "I will go no further," over another issue, earlier or later than More did. But he *chose*. It was not the intrinsic necessity of events that forced him to draw the line at this point, but it was a necessity for him as an ethical man to pick his breaking point and to stay by his decision. Here his imperative was a negative one, but like positive decisions, it bore within it some elements of the arbitrary. He had to choose.

In his novel, *Cry, The Beloved Country*, Alan Paton relates the conviction of a young White, Arthur Jarvis:

Therefore I shall devote myself, my time, my energy, my talents, to the service of South Africa. I shall no longer ask myself if this or that is expedient, but only if it is right. I shall do this, not because I am noble or unselfish, but because life slips away and because I need for the rest of my journey a star that will not play false to me, a compass that will not lie. I shall do this, not because I am a negrophile and a hater of my own, but because I cannot find it in me to do anything else. I am lost when I balance this against that, I am lost when I ask if this is safe, I am lost when I ask if men, white men or black men, Englishmen or Afrikaners, Gentiles or Jews, will approve. Therefore I shall try to do what is right, and to speak what is true.

I do this not because I am courageous and honest, but because it is the only way to end the conflict of my deepest soul. I do it because I am no longer able to aspire to the highest with one part of myself, and to deny it with another. I do not wish to live like that. I understand better those who have died for their convictions, and have not thought it as wonderful or brave or noble to die. They died rather than live, that was all. [1]

Jesus' own career embodies such an imperative. It was at the arrest of John that he chose to inaugurate his public preaching. As a young man in his early 30's (according to the gospels; Irenaeus offers strong evidence he was in his early 40's), he might well have made the decision earlier or later or

[1](New York: Scribner's, 1948), p. 175

differently. Nor need he have gone so quickly, within the year, to press the challenge home in Jerusalem. But thus he chose, and saw his decision so merged with the Father's call that on the eve of his arrest he could see his death, not simple as his own freely accepted task, but as the cup being given him to drink.

Like Dooley, More, Jarvis, Jesus, we are all commanded to command ourselves, to make the decisive choices that will make us men of fullest stature, to take the responsibility for our own ethical destiny. In this sense, all morality is deeply personal.

Hilaire Belloc put it thus in a letter to Lady Lovat:

> I have desired all the time to clarify and write down for you — for the little it may be worth as service — what seems in my mind in the matter of Decisions. They are taken but rarely in one human life, and these points would seem to be true of each and all.
>
> First, that when a true Decision is come to, there has been a full conjunction of the intelligence and the will: that is why Decisions of gravity are rare. Therefore a Decision is a thing reached by sufficient weighing of conditions and its acceptation by the will ratifies that. Every Decision of consequence has grave evils attached to it — or grave risk of evil. We deliberately conclude that the good prevails. In most Decisions there is a great act of merit.
>
> Next there is in any such Decision Peace. Full Peace is not attainable in this life, and the degree of Peace one attains is conditioned by things we cannot foretell: health and accident and the rest. But the contrast lies between the measure of Peace and the tendency to further Peace which a Decision produces, and the increasing lack of Peace which a failure to decide produces — still more a

Decision on the wrong side and for the wrong motive.

Next a Decision bears two kinds of fruit, outwards and inwards — outwards, it does good in its effect on all around us: inwards, it fructifies and increases what is in ourselves.

I think when people come to die it is not so much the memory of good deeds that can support them as the memory of Decisions taken.

They are the structure of perseverance. They are creative. And they are in communion with the ruling and directive power of Almighty God.

So they seem to me. And no matter what the unforeseen connections and effects in the future they are never really regretted in the core of the heart.[2]

The larger and more effectual moral decisions are often not those which draw the line between right and wrong, but those which choose among a wide array of alternatives. For this kind of choice one relies less upon the tradition; here morality is not so much discovered as it is created. One's configuration of ethical decisions will be as peculiarly personal as his face and fingerprints.

In passing, I would note that the partisans of situation ethics have confused these two modes of moral choice. They have tried to intrude the arbitrary and decisional postures whereby we choose between good alternatives into the process for discriminating between good and evil, where the good really is to be found, rather than picked.

To Grow Is Not To Depend Upon Society

Let me come at this individual side of ethics from a somewhat different direction. As a rule, the nobler ethical

[2]*Letters from Hilaire Belloc*, ed. Robert Speaight (London: Hollis & Carter, 1958), pp. 214-15. Letter dated August 8, 1930.

systems that have been devised by men have required *equity*. They call on men to share their substance with their fellows, to support justice, to create an equality of necessities and of opportunity among men. They are, further, ethics of *reciprocity*. They provide a pattern of conduct which, if followed mutually by other men, would enable all to live in tranquillity. They are, in fact, paradigms for reconstructing *society*. Most ethics are minimal requirements for a congenial public order, to be agreed upon by all members of society, required of all, and enforced even by coercion in cases of default.

In contrast with these ethics of equity, reciprocity, and society Jesus (differing even from his late master John) preaches a way of life that ignores equity, does not expect to find reciprocity, and could never serve as a formula to be accepted or imposed within a society. Jesus (like Marx) shows deep moral concern for the inequalities of material wherewithal. Curiously, however, he frets for the rich man perhaps even more than for the brother whom he is impoverishing. His goal is not simply an equitable redistribution of all wealth, but the saving of the precious person of every man. It is in caring for others that both rich and poor are saved, but the sharing of goods and services becomes transfigured as the sacrament of a more valuable inner exchange (unknown to Marx).

In most ethical systems good men must provide for their own protection, knowing that not all men are good, nor are any men always good. Thus the state is founded with force and maintained by it. In order to make room for the good man, the exploiter must be restrained. Jesus, on the contrary, suggests no defense against injustice, and his own experience is put forth as a clear warning to any disciple that he may expect to be exploited, and should provide for it (believing that this submission is often the only means of touching the heart of the exploiter).

A social ethic is realizable only in a society that has

already accepted it. A man will devote himself to working for justice in the hope that one day it will become the working relationship between men, that one day he may trust his neighbor and count on finding honesty and integrity from him, and thus be able, in the reconstructed society, finally to relax and be his better self. But Jesus talks little indeed about a reformed society or a better world. He insists that man save his soul right now in the most ruthless of all worlds.

The Christian ethic has customarily been disparaged as Utopian. "It would be wonderful if people could be counted upon to live that way, but of course they never will." Of course not! This, however, is to misconstrue. Jesus never suggested that it would take over the world. The kingdom — God's rule — is no social order to wait for; it is the conversion experience and love affair with the Father available to any man in this world right now. The gospel is not addressed to all men; it is addressed to any man. The believer rejoices at comradeship of belief from others, but never expects to find much. As for drawing other comrades to his side, he hopes to do this by his own example, rather than by reorganizing society.

Ironically, the ethic of Jesus Christ is the most un-Utopian in sight, ready to be lived in any circumstances whatever. To be reconciled to the Lord means to dedicate oneself against suffering and injustice, but simultaneously to live and thrive amid them. As a colleague, Robert Rodes, has written:

> I have little understanding and no hope at all except in the passion, death and resurrection of Jesus Christ, true God and true man. Not that the world lacks elements of intelligibility and elements of hopefulness; but absent the passion, death and resurrection of Jesus Christ, they fall short of unifying into an intelligible or a hopeful whole. The world presents itself neither as totally random

nor as systematically malevolent, but as a thing of flawed intelligibility, the product of frustrated benevolence. The classic problem of evil — if God could accomplish so much, why could He not have gone the rest of the way and produced a perfect creation along the lines already laid down? Intellectually, He has scant comfort for those who ask that question. . . .God has offered only one answer to the evil in the world — to undergo it Himself. Whatever in this flawed universe challenges man's understanding or belies man's hope, that God took upon Himself through His incarnation in Jesus Christ, and brought to a happy issue through His resurrection from the dead.[3]

The invitation by Jesus to death and resurrection is given to men most personally. It is a call to conversion, and as was said earlier, men may be converted in groups, yet no group was ever converted. Only persons are Christians, not groups. When one makes the commitment to spend his entire strength in service of his brothers, he cannot expect the world to reply in kind. He makes a lonely choice. He may group together with others of similar belief and like promises, yet no group has the soul or the history that an individual has.

In a sense, the world has no ethical history in the way that a single person can. There are no moments of radical transformation. Some particular project may be attempted and succeed. Racial integration may indeed be pushed through the legislatures and the courts even into people's hearts. Freedom of the press, surely of high moral value, can be established in a world where before it did not exist. Security for orphans can be provided, or women's suffrage,

---

[3]From an unpublished manuscript. "The Bride from the Desert," quoted by permission of the author.

or protection for mine workers. But as each real social achievement is realized, the selfish and predatory forces dark and deep within human hearts inevitably move to find other avenues of exploitation. Improvements must be fought for, and they mark real progress. But despite them all we cannot speak of constant moral growth among society. An individual man may have his entire life turned inside out morally, and may be radically transformed on different occasions throughout his lifetime. Not so a society, not so the world. Global history does not allow of the startling transfiguration that a single man may experience between birth and death. Thus the Christian must pursue his purposes on his own, without waiting for the world to become receptive to them. For the world remains ever the same.

The Christian churches despise their Marxist rivals for wanting to transform society through violence. Justice and peace are hardly to be established worldwide by slaughter and deceit. But has Christian experience been any more capable than Marxist theory? The Philemons of this world will be deceived by any Utopianism, ruthless or compassionate, which bids them turn their energies towards the abolition of slavery before making a brother of Onesimus.

These, then, are aspects of morality which are inescapably individual. The single person must make critical choices in the solitude of his own conscience, and cannot expect society around him to be virtuous, so that his own integrity may come easily.

The gospel is no call, however, to isolate oneself or to provide for one's individual integrity in private. It flings the believer into social service, assures him he will cleave to the Father only by succoring his brothers, and urges him to make common cause with all possible men in order to serve an ever-widening range of brothers. One is indeed to collaborate, not simply with those who have the same vision and beliefs, but with all men of good will.

In any task-group he enters, the Christian must realize

that his personal goals and those of the group cannot — must not — coincide. The group must work for equity, protect itself, and seek to re-organize society. It must coerce, must sometimes subordinate personal interests to financial need, must pursue short-term goals. The Christian can neither despise group endeavor nor impose his personal ethic upon it. Just as there is no ethical code that can contain the full force of the call of Christ, yet we must always be asking ourselves what is right and wrong; so there is no group or group activity that can contain and represent the full force of a believer's dedication and interests (not even a family, nor even a church), yet all believers must be ever working for their own goals in various groups.

This creates particular frustrations for any person holding public office: stateswoman, churchman, corporation executive, or mother of a family. One is caught both ways. On the one hand, since any group moves but by consensus, the public officer is often held back by the sluggishness and faltering motives of his colleagues, and drawn to compromise and bite his lip. On the other hand, so much of his energies and ego are thrown into public leadership that he is tempted to submerge all his personal growth into the projects at hand, and to reserve no identity for himself other than his public person. The service of men requires many public officers, but none more than they must work out their salvation in fear and trembling. Not a few such men have been beguiled understandably into thinking that they were laying down their lives for their brother, while in fact they were suffering instead the loss of their own souls.

Thus far, in exploring the ethical relationship between person and society, I have argued that the irreducible unit of moral concern is the single person, not society. It is the single man and woman that must make his or her own ethical decisions; and these decisions are largely for that same individual self. It is the person that loves, and lives beyond death; no society is capable of either. This is one reason why

Christians have ever shied away from princes and politics that
wished to claim their total loyalty, and why they have held
their own churchmen in highest contempt when they
corrupted the Church into a self-serving or totalitarian
organization.

To Grow Is To Reckon With Society

But now, to turn the corner into another avenue of
discussion, I want to stress the fact that the individual
person, if he is to grow and mature into love, is obliged to
turn his care and service towards society.

The newly born child begins in utter selfishness. If
original sin has any meaning, it would reside neither in some
hereditary curse spoken of by many of the Church Fathers,
nor in the latent youthful savagery depicted by William
Golding in *Lord of the Flies*. It is the thorough egocentricity
in which we all are born, and from which we must, at our
peril, grow. The child becomes a man as he encounters and
comes to terms successively with parents, siblings, playmates
and friends, teachers, spouse, children, professional asso-
ciates. One's life widens as one comes to care for ever
widening circles of people. One becomes a full-grown
individual to the extent that one is socialized.

But this is not enough. In life's course it is possible to
become attached only to those who in some way belong to
one, who can be trusted, who can be counted on. In a word,
one can limit love to those who offer a return. There is
another step we must take, if we are not always to remain
held by the aboriginal selfishness: to reach out in love to the
stranger. In the Old Testament the test case of sincere love
was the "sojourner in the land". Every village might have a
few Gentile members, resident or passing through: not kin of
the tribe or the nation, but thrown upon the hospitality of a
people who for survival had had to be wary of any alien folk.
Yet the token of unselfish love was to take care of the

sojourner, who offered no *quid pro quo*. In the New
Testament the test case is one's enemy. If the believer could
bring himself to forgive and even to cherish the man who
sought only the believer's harm, then one had true love. If I
could suggest a test case for our own time, it would be the
anonymous man, the unknown and unmet citizen, the public.

Recently the concern over environmental devastation
has brought to our attention the way we have of mistreating
the environment, in a way we would never treat private
property. Ecologists accuse us of the "downstream mental-
ity", a willingness to discard our own offal without regard for
whomever it will then afflict. The acrid smokestacks of Gary,
the vanishing game preserves of Africa, the strip-mined
wastelands of Kentucky, and the slimy pollution of the
Thames all testify to our contempt for the anonymous man.

Being an academic, I see the same thing on a minute but
vexing scale at the university. The first week of every
academic year, students arrive and work industriously to
furnish and brighten their rooms. Mothers come with
matching bedspreads and curtains; sons repaint the walls; the
Salvation Army provides worn-out refrigerators. There is
always much carpentry, and I notice year after year that for
an entire week the hallways are littered with piles of sawdust
and wood scraps and trash, while the rooms themselves are
made attractive. I am reminded of more primitive cities
where the citizens all empty their chamber pots from the
windows into the street each morning. Evidently the corri-
dor, belonging to everyone, is seen to belong to no one in
particular, and thus becomes a dump, a no-man's land.

One must have a sense of proportion. It is not exactly
the same thing when a motorist flips his cigarette butt out
the window onto the roadside; or when 36 people watch Kitty
Genovese being stabbed to death in Kew Gardens in open
daylight, and no one either shouts, stops the assailant, or
moves to call for help; or when 40% of the registered voters
fail to cast their ballots in a national election; or a nation

does not much notice that women are ripping their undesired children from their wombs by the hundreds of thousands. But the slant of mind is the same. We are sensitive to those who are known to us, but easily de-personalize the faceless man, the neighbor. We all walk briskly along the road from Jerusalem to Jericho, glancing neither to right nor to left.

Governments in our day have assumed new obligations to succor the warstricken, to supply help in national disasters, to support the impoverished. But we are easily drugged by the presence of the government and the existence of so many social enterprises. Somehow we have managed to shift all responsibility for need beyond our immediate reach to officials and organizations. And thus we are morally dwarfed. It is surely ironic that in the very age when citizens have insisted that their governments be more active in socially constructive activity, individuals have been encouraged to transfer any long-distance moral responsibility to appropriate agencies, and to return into their social torpor, caring not for those who never come into personal touch with them. In this sense, increased socialism has anaesthetized social concern in the hearts of men. And without this loving and active service of those who are neither close enough nor well-enough disposed to scratch one's back in return, no man can rise out of his original sin, no man will have left land, house, and kin to follow Jesus.

One would perhaps have expected some counter-poising emphasis upon social duty in our time from the moral theologians, but there are even here some grounds from complaint, which I should like to explore.

Sexuality And Force

Reading over contemporary literature in the field of ethics leads one to discover that most of the illustrations and topics of interest derive from the twin areas of sex and violence. What are the debated issues of the day? Contraception, extra-

and pre-marital intercourse, homosexuality, divorce, abortion, nuclear armaments, conscientious objection, and the like. Perhaps there is something more significant reflected here than that native human prurience that has ever had its fascination tickled by sex and violence.

In the thirteenth century Aquinas commented upon the curious resemblances between what he called the concupiscible and the irascible appetites, which we would call sex drive and wrath. Freud as a young man at first identified libido and aggression, on ground that they were alternate expressions of one basic drive for sexual mastery over others. In his later career, however, he preferred to differentiate them, in the belief that libidinal drive seeks after life, but aggressive drive is death-oriented. While not perhaps identifying them, I would agree with the younger Freud and with Thomas that they are curiously comparable. "The vicissitudes of aggression resemble those of sexuality to such a degree that the assumption of a constant driving power comparable to that of libido seems appropriate."[4]

One feature they obviously have in common is that they both involve physical contact: one must somehow touch the body of another, whether to caress or to assault. These are among man's deepest and most direct relations. In their simplest forms they bring persons into one-to-one confrontation, body-to-body (or, when awry, body-against-body) encounter.

The ethical discussion surrounding these two behavior areas has, it seems, focused upon just this individual aspect, while ignoring possible social implications. Considerations of thermo-nuclear weaponry, for instance, document vividly what becomes of the citizens upon whom the bomb falls. Why not

---

[4]Heinz Hartmann, Ernst Kris, and Rudolph M. Loewenstein, "Notes on the Theory of Aggression, *"Papers on Psychoanalytic Psychology: Psychological Issues,* IV, 2 (Monograph 14), 1964, p. 78.

reckon with equal vividness what becomes of the politics and economics of nations that invest heavily in weapons which may never even be used? Many writers are distressed over the abrupt increase in teenage pregnancy and VD, without looking beyond it to the decay of the family that gives children little strength to hunger for something deeper than cheap intimacy. Treatises on the just war theory take for their model a situation in which one innocent citizen is attacked on the street by another. Defensive intervention on the victim's behalf is justified, and then the miniature model is immediately projected to national scale. This may have been more allowable when wars were essentially private struggles between princes. But today the one-to-one model simply does not serve to resolve ethical problems that are of national and world size.

This lack of interest in the rights and wrongs of social involvement desensitizes one to the massive values of good and evil that resist being reduced to a simple, person-to-person dimension. To understand sex, one must inquire not simply into the proprieties of genital intercourse, but also into the different possibilities of marital fidelity, the rearing of children, the loyalty to kin and clan and town and people which the ancients called *pietas,* the public status of women, caring for elder grandparents, the conflict of prolonged irresponsibility caused by lengthened education far past the marrying age, and so many other broad issues. Violent force would become an expanded notion, touching upon slum landlordism, election fraud, international trade imbalances, racial segregation, malnutrition, and so forth. One would think of violence, not as limited to the simple model of physical assault, but of whatever *violates* integrity. I would propose the term "isometric violence", to depict the brutal, unyielding shove that destroys persons, though no one is struck or bruised, no one dies, no one is buried.

Ethics returns by preference to the paradigmatic problems that deceive, for the really ponderable issues are more tricky, and are neglected. Theologians, for instance, are reluctant to scrutinize restraint of trade by labor unions, manipulation of motivation through advertizing, increasing monopolies in the communications media, expanding inequities in international development, wastage and pollution of natural resources, inertia in prison reform. Moral comment has been in the grip of what can only be called a sort of selfishness. We have bothered ourselves with good and evil, but no further than one could touch and see and hear. Our values are all writ small. We have given our attention to close, person-to-person behavior, and ignored the social structures, massive pressures, and intricate commitments that also make us the persons we are.

If I may recur once again to the concerns of sex and of force, there is a noticeable preference in our time to make more absolute judgments about them. Curiously, liberal moralists lean towards the opinion that almost all sexual activity is good, while almost every use of force is evil. Surely this slide towards facile judgments also demonstrates that the issues are viewed more in their simple, individual dimensions, than in their admittedly more diffuse, but very meaningful social effects.

Conscientious Objector or Conscientious Warrior

After these general observations on the individual and social aspects of Christian ethics, let us turn to a consideration of particulars. My main concern being to identify and comment upon the more general conclusions for ethics which would follow from a refreshed Christian theology, I have refrained from inquiry into any particular moral issues. By way of illustration, however, I should like to deal with one normative question, in order both to illustrate what I have in mind by way of a proper approach, and to see whether this approach, simultaneously individual and social, may consistently and usefully serve in the resolution of particular problems. The issue in question is the proper use of force. More particularly, should one acquiesce in armed warfare, or should he refuse to take up arms for any cause whatever? The question is alive in our times, and illustrative of problems that are in every time alive.

It is fair to admit that the gospel represents Jesus as biased against all use of force, and that he raises the issue explicitly in the context of defense. If a man is bent on robbing you of your goods, present them to him as a gift rather than resisting. If he would have your coat, then let him have your shirt as well. Evil, he advises, is best not met with evil, but with guileless good, that can eventually wear down the evil. On the eve of his own arrest he tells his own following to put away weapons, for he who takes up the sword will die by it. Since he was himself on his way to death, one infers that it is not the risk of falling by the opponent's sword he warns of, but the risk of losing one's soul by the sword in his own hand. More vividly than by words, though, he demonstrates by his acceptance of arrest, torture, and execution that his source of power lies not in coercion or force, but in his powerlessness. Only by dying in his innocence can he reach the violent hearts of those who assassinate him. Thus by dying, not by killing, does he overcome death. He cares not to defend himself or his followers. It is not they who need help, but those who have murder in their hearts, and they can only be overpowered by one who does not meet them on their ground.

Christians during the first two or three centuries tended to refuse military service in the empire. It seems that this was not from any conviction — held individually or shared throughout the community of believers — that it was evil to bear arms. But at this period a soldier was required, in his induction oath, to offer worship to the emperor as god.

This explains why a Christian would bridle at entering the emperor's service, but it also suggests what might be an objection to any military enterprise. In a sense, the allegiance which any effective military commander must exact comes very close to the fidelity of divine worship. Surely one of the first objections one would raise to armed service, even in the absence of conflict, is that a man must surrender one of his most human prerogatives: that of evaluating orders and deciding what he will do. To be sure, most military regimes do in theory allow members of the armed forces to resist orders deemed immoral, but in practice no army can tolerate resistant decision-making. The force of an army is massed within its unity: immense numbers of men marching to single orders. The very need in an army for unquestioning obedience may represent its most dehumanizing effect, even without combat.

One might also consider the simple effects of carrying a weapon. There is a marked difference in bearing, for example, between a policeman in America and a Bobby in Great Britain. Being unarmed, a Bobby is at all times thrown upon his nerve and wit and muscle. Whether he chases a burglar or tries to restrain a tipsy crowd, he must come to terms with people. But a man who carries a weapon, particularly an exposed weapon, expects to be able to command and subdue anyone in sight, or any crowd. With the best of intentions, one easily develops a sort of moral swagger, a feeling that one never need come to terms with an opponent. I do not ignore that the kinds of violence the ordinary urban police officer confronts are more savage in America than in Britain. But the point remains: one who constantly carries a weapon easily picks up an arrogance which is only intensified if he is himself under constant orders, and needing others to have the mastery over.

Perhaps it is not death itself that is the blackest flower of war. Those who neither stand nor fall in battle, but have taken up arms and assumed the force that their mere threat offers, invite another form of destruction:

> Here [in death on the battlefield] we see
> force in its grossest and most summary form — the

force that kills. How much more varied in its processes, how much more surprising in its effects is the other force, the force that does *not* kill, i.e., that does not kill just yet. It will surely kill, it will possibly kill, or perhaps it merely hangs, poised and ready, over the head of the creature it *can* kill, at any moment, which is to say at every moment. In whatever aspect, its effect is the same: it turns a man into a stone. From its first property (the ability to turn a human being into a thing by the simple method of killing him) flows another, quite prodigious too in its way, the ability to turn a human being into a thing while he is still alive. He is alive; he has a soul; and yet — he is a thing.[5]

These words of Simone Weil, a young French Jewess, commenting upon the *Illiad* in the warstricken world of Europe in 1940, introduce what may be one of the most sensitive studies of warfare written in our time. Her theme is not unlike that of Jesus, who warned men they would die by picking up the sword. "Force," she writes, "is as pitiless to the man who possesses it, or thinks he does, as it is to its victims; the second it crushes, the first it intoxicates. The truth is, nobody really possesses it."[6]

It is the strong man, she observes, who can be most overcome by force:

The man who is the possessor of force seems to walk through a non-resistant element; in the human substance that surrounds him nothing has the power to interpose, between the impulse and the act, the tiny interval that is reflection. When

[5]*The Iliad, or the Poem of Force,* Trans. Mary McCarthy (Wallingford, Pa.: Pendle Hill, 1956), pp. 4-5.

[6]*Ibid.,* p. 11.

there is no room for reflection, there is none either
for justice or prudence.[7]

The intoxication of battle creates a momentum which
cannot be stopped, an exhilaration in combat that forgets its
own purposes, if ever it had any.

At the time their own destruction seems
impossible to them. For they do not see that the
force in their possession is only a limited quantity;
nor do they see their relations with other human
beings as a kind of balance between unequal
amounts of force. Since other people do not
impose on their movements that halt, that interval
of hesitation, wherein lies all our consideration for
our brothers in humanity, they conclude that
destiny has given complete license to them, and
none at all to their inferiors. . .

Thus war effaces all conceptions of purpose
or goal, including even its own "war aims." It
effaces the very notion of war's being brought to
an end. To be outside a situation so violent as this
is to find it inconceivable; to be inside it is to be
unable to conceive its end. Consequently, nobody
does anything to bring this end about. In the
presence of an armed enemy, what hand can
relinquish its weapon? The mind ought to find a
way out, but the mind has lost all capacity to so
much as look forward. The mind is completely
absorbed in doing itself violence. Always in human
life, whether war or slavery is in question, intolerable sufferings continue, as it were, by the force of
their own specific gravity, and so look to the
outsider as though they were easy to bear; actually
they continue because they have deprived the

[7]*Ibid.*, pp. 13-14.

sufferer of the resources which might have served to extricate him... If the existence of an enemy has made a soul destroy in itself the thing nature put there, then the only remedy the soul can imagine is the destruction of the enemy...

Such is the nature of force. Its power of converting a man into a thing is a double one, and in its application double-edged. To the same degree, though in different fashions, those who use it and those who endure it are turned to stone. This property of force achieves its maximum effectiveness during the clash of arms, in battle, when the tide of the day has turned, and everything is rushing toward a decision. It is not the planning man, the man of strategy, the man acting on the resolution taken, who wins or loses a battle; battles are fought and decided by men deprived of these faculties, men who have undergone a transformation, who have dropped either to the level of inert matter, which is pure passivity, or to the level of blind force, which is pure momentum.[8]

In war, the misfortune of the victims and casualties is obvious. Weil is at pains to notice the price paid by those who win. It is the wantonness and abandon that destroy even the conqueror, she says. The very use of arms summons up a fury which quickly escapes one's original purposes.

"A moderate use of force, which alone would enable man to escape being enmeshed in its machinery, would require superhuman virtue, which is as rare as dignity in weakness."[9] Moderation is possible but evaporates so easily.

[8]*Ibid.*, pp. 14, 22, 23, 25-26. See also J. Glenn Gray, *The Warriors: Reflections on Men in Battle* (New York: Harcourt, Brace, & Co., 1959. Also published in a Harper Torchbook edition).

[9]*Ibid.*, p. 19.

The forces of sex and anger in man are fueled by deep and smoldering passions. Provided these passions be absorbed into one's purposes, provided they be held by temperance so that one acts from the core of his being, love and fidelity are only magnified by carnal ecstacy, and wrath and indignation find stronger voice in force and temper. They are risky but humane forces. It is when they pick up a speed of their own, when intemperance causes sex and anger to arise, no longer from within the depths of the soul, but with an irrational and berserk fury (this word equally describes both lechery and violence), that a man is at the mercy of his own passions. Thus even the most sincere and self-sacrificing defender of an unjustly exploited neighbor must realize that if he rise to arms to put down an aggressor, the arms may turn upon him if he not have that "superhuman virtue" which can allow him to survive.

The problem of the soldier, then, may not be death endured or inflicted, so much as the destruction of all combatants by bestial fury. Warfare in a just cause provides just that excitement which will allow the beast inside to crawl out unnoticed. It is not so much the war itself, as what war summons out from within us.

This is well put by James Goldman's *The Lion in Winter*, in an exchange between the queen and one of her truculent sons.

> ### Richard the Lionhearted
> A knife. He's got a knife [refers to his brother John].
>
> #### Eleanor of Aquitaine [their Mother]
> Of course, he has a knife. He always has a knife. We all have knives.
>
> It is eleven eighty-three and we're barbarians. How clear we make it.
>
> Oh, my piglets, we're the origins of war. Not history's forces nor the times nor justice nor the

lack of it nor causes nor religions nor ideas nor
kinds of government nor any other thing.
We are the killers; we breed war.
We carry it, like syphilis, inside.
Dead bodies rot in field and stream because
the living ones are rotten.
For the love of God, can't we love one
another just a little?
That's how peace begins. We have so much to
love each other for. We have such possibilities, my
children. We could change the world.[10]

To be ready to enter wholeheartedly into the violence
of war, a man must shut down his normal sensitivities. Oddly
enough, one of the effects of unleashed fury is a numbness to
fellow-humans, a nonchalance about death and agony. One
must be able to look upon global disaster and writhing
suffering with placidity. That is, one must not look at them
at all. Upon his retirement from the U.S. Air Force in 1966,
General Paul Tibbets, pilot of the *Enola Gay*, the aircraft
which dropped the first atomic bomb upon Hiroshima,
commented: "I look back on it purely as a job I was assigned
to do. We knew the effects that bomb would have when we
dropped it. We looked down from the plane and we could see
the havoc it was making. Of course I think it was right to
drop the bomb. I don't think about the effects of it, though.
If you start doing that you would go insane."[11]

Simone Weil points out the growing purposelessness that
grows out of combat. To start with, one may have a cause to
fight for, and a sense of its worth. But in the course of
conflict, both cause and perspective yield to an obstinate and

[10](New York: Dell, 1968), pp. 77-78.

[11]"A-Bomb pilot No. 1 calls it a day", Mileva Ross, *The Sunday Express*
[London], August 7, 1956, p. 7.

blinded determination to vanquish, with the why's and the what's and the who's no longer in sight. I cannot refrain from quoting here a somewhat extended passage from *The Spy Who Came in from the Cold,* by John le Carré, for it embodies much of the sense of what Weil was trying to convey. The hero, a British agent named Leamas, has been captured by communists in East Germany, and is being interrogated by Fiedler, his captor.

> Most of all [Fiedler] asked about their philosophy.
>
> To Leamas that was the most difficult question of all.
>
> "What do you mean, a philosophy?" he replied; "we're not Marxists, we're nothing. Just people."
>
> "Are you Christians, then?"
>
> "Not many, I shouldn't think. I don't know many."
>
> "What makes them do it, then?" Fiedler persisted; "they must have a philosophy."
>
> "Why must they? Perhaps they don't know; don't even care. Not everyone has a philosophy," Leamas answered, a little helplessly.
>
> "Then tell me what is your philosophy?"
>
> "Oh for Christ's sake," Leamas snapped, and they walked on in silence for a while. But Fiedler was not to be put off.
>
> "If they do not know what they want, how can they be so certain they are right?"
>
> "Who the hell said they were?" Leamas replied irritably.
>
> "But what is the justification then? What is it? For us it is easy, as I said to you last night. The Abteilung and organisations like it are the natural extension of the Party's arm. They are in the

vanguard of the fight for Peace and Progress. They are to the party what the party is to socialism: they *are* the vanguard. Stalin said so" — he smiled drily, "it is not fashionable to quote Stalin — but he said once 'half a million liquidated is a statistic, and one man killed in a traffic accident is a national tragedy.' He was laughing, you see, at the bourgeois sensitivities of the mass. He was a great cynic. But what he meant is still true: a movement which protects itself against counter-revolution can hardly stop at the exploitation — or the elimination, Leamas — of a few individuals. It is all one, we have never pretended to be wholly just in the process of rationalising society. Some Roman said it, didn't he, in the Christian Bible — it is expedient that one man should die for the benefit of many."

"I expect so," Leamas replied wearily.

"Then what do you think? What is your philosophy?"

"I just think the whole lot of you are bastards," said Leamas savagely.

Fiedler nodded. "That is a viewpoint I understand. It is primitive, negative and very stupid — but it is a viewpoint, it exists. But what about the rest of the [agents] ?"

"I don't know. How should I know?"

"Have you never discussed philosophy with them?"

"No. We're not Germans." He hesitated, then added vaguely: "I suppose they don't like Communism."

"And that justifies, for instance, the taking of human life? That justifies the bomb in the crowded restaurant; that justifies your write-off rate of agents — all that?"

Leamas shrugged. "I suppose so."

"You see, for us it does," Fiedler continued, "I myself would have put a bomb in a restaurant if it brought us further along the road. Afterwards I would draw the balance — so many women, so many children; and so far along the road. But Christians — and yours is a Christian society — Christians may not draw the balance."

"Why not. They've got to defend themselves, haven't they?"

"But they believe in the sanctity of life. They believe every man has a soul which can be saved. They believe in sacrifice."

"I don't know. I don't much care," Leamas added. "Stalin didn't either, did he?"

Fiedler smiled; "I like the English," he said, almost to himself; "my father did too. He was very fond of the English."

"That gives me a nice, warm feeling," Leamas retorted, and relapsed into silence.[12]

Perhaps even more clearly than the soldier, the spy becomes an operative of the uninhibited struggle between nations.

In the world which the spy inhabits, there is no such thing as a friendly nation. In the main, the world of nations is a pagan world, expressing no ethic except that of individual survival. It is dark and cold out there, and nothing grows save suspicion and fear. . .

A voluntary exile from the organized body of society, the spy is supposed to divest himself of every tenet of the ethic except loyalty. This

[12](London: The Reprint Society, 1964), pp. 133-35.

loyalty is not really an expression of any moral obligation, however; it is merely, like expendability, one of the terms of employment.

What would be a foul, heartless deed for anyone else could be a matter for congratulation in a spy. Unfair, indecent, immoral? These are words for propagandists, for people inside a society. In the frozen void, the dark side of international politics, they are not words with meaning, words such as *gun* or *document* or *orders.*

"The work of an intelligence service. . .is an obscure, ungrateful work; it is composed of the sum of tasks which have about them nothing of the romantic, the amusing or the comfortable. . .

It demands an effacement of personality, a modesty and a spirit of sacrifice of which few men are capable, and of which even fewer men are capable for long."[13]

Another thing about warfare: the level of savagery is always determined by the more ruthless party. The regular armed services of the older countries, more used to war, have agreed upon the Geneva Convention. In a word, they agree not to use certain measures of cruelty only because they would rather not suffer them in return. But in the world of the spy there are no such conventions. Likewise the French army found in Algeria, when it confronted a determined population led by nationalist guerillas, it had to meet the Algerians, atrocity for atrocity, until the army discovered with loathing what it had become, and many regular soldiers simply revolted against descending any lower into butchery.

Perhaps this is the point we have been trying to explore

[13]Blake Ehrlich, *Resistance: France 1940-45* (New York: The New American Library [Signet Books], 1966), pp. 106-107. He quotes from Col. Georges Groussard, *Service secret* (Paris, 1964).

regarding the bearing of arms. Once the temple of Mars has its doors flung open, there is a god of destruction let abroad that will devastate the land and lives of all.

Jesus insists that he will be assimilated to no one, least of all to the man who takes up weapons. By succumbing to the violence of Jews and Gentiles alike, he overpowered his aggressors. Unlike the warriors who in their fury lose all sense or recollection of what they are about, he pursues his own purpose relentlessly. Perhaps the only man possessed of the "superhuman virtue" that would allow him to take up the sword without dying by it, he considers that the sword is incapable of the conquest of men's hearts, and a victory at arms would be too puny a success to merit his attention. It would indeed seem that a Christian could well choose to follow this example, rather than lose himself in war.

Now let the problem be regarded from the other side. It is quite understandable that some would seek peace through nonviolence. But what solution do they offer for the violent who, despite the best witness and example, remain bent upon exploitation, and who destroy both peace and peaceful together? Though followers of Christ may endeavor to incorporate his disdain of force and coercion into their lives, and may seek to ally like-minded comrades with them, they must never look to the day when this will be a consensual conviction of society. It is a stance of high virtue, and this will never be a majority phenomenon. We may always count on the presence of energetic and aggressive men who will victimize and oppress and destroy their neighbors.

One of the services of government is to contain these voracious men. It is the aim of the virtuous to convert the voracious, but one must always realize that they will in large part fail of their aim. Meanwhile, the society creates for itself a government that is founded upon force.[14] Let there be no

---

[14]See the very interesting remarks by Jacques Ellul in *Violence: Reflections from a Christian Perspective* (New York: Seabury, 1969), pp. 84-88.

mistake: a law is not simply a declaration of what the society deems ethical, but a proclamation of the terms on which coercion and punishment will be applied. Coercion admittedly never reaches down to the roots of evil; thus we speak of the public agencies as only containing the victim-izers, and protecting that modicum of peace which allows men to apply other, more potent remedies to their fellows.

The tasks and resources of the state are admittedly limited, and so much the better that this is agreed. James Schall writes:

> There is evil in the world; we must confront it somehow in an organized way. When we withdraw from the present civil order on the grounds that it is totally corrupt, that no process of the liberal state will really work, or when we, more logically perhaps, seek to create a totally new order with none of the defects of the human reality, when, in short, we render also unto God the things that are Ceasar's, we have already taken the leap into the greatest of the social confusions, we have already crossed over the great dividing line that separates this world from the next.[15]

Neither law nor force can establish tranquillity of the heart, nor should it be the ambition of the state to do so. But it can strive to hold victimizers sufficiently at bay to permit men to work for that further peace which neither the state nor indeed the world can give.

It is important to see that this is a common good. When a man walks down Main Street on a dark night and is mugged, that may simply be a matter of his head and his pocket cash. But if matters on Main Street are at such a pass that a man often does get mugged, or is likely to get mugged,

---

[15]James V. Schall, S.J., "Caesar as God," *Commonweal*, February 6, 1970, p. 507.

then Main Street is effectively removed from public use. It is
a deprivation for everyone, whether or not anyone actually
braves the street and makes his way from end to end with his
head intact. What the public needs is to be able to count on
Main Street being safe. And they need to be able to count on
their medicines being pure, their drinking water uncon-
taminated, their traffic predictable, their basic commodities
purchasable, fire protection available, foreign travel protected, bank drafts honored, children unmolested. Briefly, every
man needs to be able to enjoy a certain calculable trust in his
neighbors, to know that in a minimal way he is protected
from molestation. He needs to be free from consuming all his
attention and temper in defending himself and his own; he
needs to be free of suspicion.

　　These are not simply material values of a second order,
to be disdained because they are not the goods within a
man's soul. A man with superhuman virtue, that inner peace
which permits a man to confront violence and absorb it, to
be tempered and annealed by it rather than bent or crushed
by it, may well contemplate and suffer these deprivations and
insecurities without letting them harm his soul or disturb his
peace. For a man who has not yet so composed himself in
love, but might, to live under oppression can well pierce
through his skin to the soul. Despotism can destroy both the
body and the soul in hell. If there are sacraments of grace and
love, material exchanges which enliven man's heart, there are
also sacraments of evil, material oppression and outrage that
can twist and break the human spirit.

　　Wars have been fought for so many reasons, most of
them ignoble and perfidious. But if one would seek the cause
which might most easily justify men taking up arms, it would
be the liberation of an oppressed people, whether from
exploitative rulers or from occupying aliens. And although
men can undergo victimization of various sorts and still
manage to bear it, there does seem to be a breaking point, an
explosive moment when suddenly men deem their own lives

cheap by comparison with freedom. To be sure, it is one thing to consider one's own life expendable, and quite another to call down the massive horror of war upon nations and peoples. But it is still a fact that men have deemed such monumental misery a worthwhile price to pay for freedom. As the Declaration of Independence observes:

> . . .all experience hath shown that mankind are more disposed to suffer, while evils are sufferable, than to right themselves by abolishing the forms [of government] to which they are accustomed. But when a long train of abuses and usurpations, pursuing invariably the same object, evinces a desire to reduce them under absolute despotism, it is their right, it is their duty, to throw off such government and to provide new guards for their future security.

And so many other peoples besides the colonial Americans have decided it right and dutiful to put into jeopardy their lives, their fortunes, and their sacred honor. Admittedly, mixed within their motives have been some desire for vengeance, envy for possessions, and rabid anger. But the decision has justified itself on the rational conclusion that despotism destroys the life of the spirit, and so becomes a moral evil that can be at least held at bay by physical force.

In the ordinary course of events, force exercises more influence simply by being in readiness, than by being brought into action. A police force, for instance, is far more significant for the crime which is deterred, than for the crime which it seeks to punish. So the issue of armed warfare must be pressed back to the issue of a standing armed force with dominance sufficient to restrain aggression. If one waits until the last bitter moment of abuse before acting, then it is nigh impossible to act, and the destructive force that must be unleashed has to be much more intense than had the abuse been confronted earlier. Pastor Martin Niemöller, a victim of the Nazi oppression, wrote:

> First they arrested the Communists — but I was not a Communist, so I did nothing. Then they came for the Social Democrats — but I was not a Social Democrat, so I did nothing. Then they arrested the trade unionists — and I did nothing because I was not one. And then they came for the Jews and then the Catholics, but I was neither a Jew nor a Catholic and I did nothing. At last they came and arrested me — and there was no one left to do anything about it.

There are, then, gentle and reasonable men who go to war, sadly but not grudgingly, to gain or regain a freedom which they consider as morally necessary as love. At its conclusion they visit the cemeteries with grief but without desolation, and reckon themselves and their fallen comrades as virtuous — whether or not they have reported a victory. They would consider themselves cowards and moral dwarfs had they not been willing to make the sacrifice.

Choosing Among Options

I have tried to sketch out two moral choices, as sympathetic to the one as to the other. They are options only in the sense that one must choose either one; but one *must choose*.

He may choose for armed force. The world, he observes, is infected deeply by greed and cruelty, which can rise into the tyranny that eats out men's hearts. Those who crave justice and freedom must therefore organize and hold in readiness armed forces: police within and armies for without. These they must control and wield as best they can, for they are capable of wreaking far more harm than good. Indeed, since the use of force so often has provoked incalculable harm, since most revolutions really only re-allot injustice, since most deprived groups that rise to power use it in their turn to deprive others, peoples must use their forces with forbearance and patience and fear. But force there must be. The goal of coercion is admittedly meager: to provide a public tranquillity wherein men may sleep without terror, eat the bread they earn, publish the truth, and preach and worship from their conscience. None of this is ultimately worthwhile without the deeper peace that grace brings, but for most people these freedoms are themselves the graces that make room for all others.

In quite another direction, a man may refuse to have anything to do with force. There is no evil abroad in the world that is not exceeded by the violence that is mistakenly applied as remedy. By taking up arms against the tyrant one really succumbs to his greatest threat: one agrees to become as the tyrant is. No sufficiently radical change is made in human affairs by the use of force. The only heart-deep transformation comes when men agree to renounce power, and to overcome the victimizers by being loving victims. One's brief life would be ill spent if he did not have ambitions beyond survival and public tranquillity.

The conscientious warrior and the conscientious object-or stand at great variance, yet they are also comrades. Both have chosen a pathway of service to walk upon; both are willing to follow it to death. Together they stand in almost equal opposition to the ordinary warrior, who is lost in his fury, and to the ordinary objector, who declines equally to take up arms for his neighbor or to suffer imprisonment or death as a witness to him. It requires similarly superhuman virtue to be a conscientious warrior or to be a conscientious objector. Either choice must be made with deep regard for

one's own self, and with disregard for self in service of one's
brothers. Each should regard his gift to his brothers as
invaluable, yet incomplete. Both will be held in some public
contempt, unrecognized in their respective heroism. Perhaps
only the one could understand the other.

I have taken this issue of armed warfare to illustrate the
kind of ethical decision-making that must be at once utterly
personal and expansively social. Philemon — the Christian —
must determine his own course, knowing that his overriding
concern is to grow to fullest human stature, ready to meet
the consuming love of his creator. For the large turnings of
the way, he will have some help and advice — but only
some — to help him choose the road. He must summon to
himself considerable independence, for he must become a
man in a hostile world, one which will not keep pace with
him as he grows from birth to death. Knowing well that he
can never transform men within it, he turns the brunt of his
generosity on his neighbors, reaching wider and wider from
Onesimus outward, in increasingly sensitive concern, reaching
out with his sympathy and substance to those who crave his
service. He will come to have an ethic both personal and
social, driven by an unmanageable imperative.

At the end he will wring his hands, admitting that he is
but an unprofitable servant. But at the end he knows he will
be welcomed into the kingdom.

5 The Rituals
of Jesus,
the Anti-Ritualist

The Christian vision is of a Father whose relentless love elicits a similarly relentless love from man, embodied in service of his brother. It might seem that in such a belief system, the stress upon ethics would derogate from attention to ritual. If the real business of growth from selfishness into generous love is the task of time in eternity, then worship could rather easily appear as a distraction or a diversion. Yet it is not so. The mind and conscience of Philemon — and any Christian — are stung precisely by the devout accomplishment of ritual. What is unfortunately so prone to routine can be, should be, and rightly is the believer's antidote to routine.[1]

The gospels report a curious hesitancy on the part of Jesus towards his people's worship. He was known to be meticulous about the fulfilment of temple obligations. Yet

---

[1]What follows appeared in the *Journal of the American Academy of Religion*, XXXIX, 4 (December, 1971), 513-525, and is here re-presented by permission of the editor.

when his companions newly come to town were ogling at the
new sanctuary under construction, he pooh-poohed the
temple, suggesting that many of those attending it to offer
sacrifice made a farce of the place by harboring hate in their
hearts; it would be torn down far more swiftly than it had
been built. It was common knowledge that he prayed a great
deal; in fact, he frequently annoyed his disciples by dis-
appearing into the wilderness on just those exciting occasions
when they had managed to draw a decent crowd to listen to
him. And yet when he talks about prayer his forehead
furrows, and there is a note of caution. Be careful of prayer,
he says. . .many men pray for the crowd. He gave alms; in
fact, one of the designated tasks within his group was to hold
the common purse and look after beggars and the destitute
poor. When he spoke of almsgiving, however, he had sharp
criticism for philanthropists who extended their hand only
before an appreciative audience. Regarding the priests, he
encouraged his people to do their duty by them in all correct
observance; as for their personal worth, he spoke of it only
with frowns and harsh complaint. He frequented the syna-
gogues, but was on the outs with the scribes who staffed
them.

Jesus is a regular and devout participant in all the
customary worship activities of his people. Yet he constantly
warns his followers about what a sham worship could be.
Why so? One reason is fairly obvious: worship, though
directed towards God, is done in the company of one's fellow
men. Hence a continuous temptation to play to the gallery,
to turn worship into a dramatic display intended mainly to
enhance one's public reputation.

Hypocrisy is recognized and feared in most churches as
the great spoiler of worship. But there is another characteristic of cult which is well received within most religious
traditions, though it runs clean athwart the purpose and
policies of Jesus Christ. It is this: Worship is seen as a

symbolic submission to the service of God, as the chief means of reconciling believers and their Lord. It is at worship that men meet God, appeal to him, have explicit and articulate interchange with him, have their offenses lifted, and make their peace with him. Worship is the occasion to turn aside from the affairs of men, to treat directly with the Lord.

One cannot deny that this view would be at home in most Christian assemblies. But I submit that it conflicts with the insights from the gospel elaborated earlier in this book. Firstly, if Jesus reveals a Father whose acceptance of us is perpetual, we need no ceremonies to draw him to us, to atone, to merit his good pleasure. And if we grow to respond to his love by costful service of our neighbor — especially our needy neighbor — then no prayers or rites whatever could take the place of this service.

Ritual as Distasteful

Thus there are two misunderstandings. It has ever been a temptation for Christians to consider ethics as a means of changing God; by proper behavior one would win the divine favor. The same temptation is endemic to worship: men would use it to turn God's head, to abate his wrath. One would effectively disbelieve what Christians must believe: that the Father can but love us. The second misunderstanding is that the disciplined and energetic conduct whereby one grows to be a loving man can somehow be replaced by worship. It is this twofold twist — that worship can manipulate God, and obviates ethics — which makes for magic.

There is in our time a noticeable disaffection for worship in various world faiths, especially Christianity. One very obvious cause for the decline is that, as a general rule, most worship is lousy. In Church one hears songs bawled with words which, if anyone fastened his attention on them with much care, would seem embarrassingly insipid. Prayers are uttered in a style that does not often rise above that of the late Cardinal Cushing's less fortunate civic invocations. Amongst all genres of human discourse, perhaps no other is less intelligent or communicative than the sermon. J. F. Powers writes, "I myself have suffered all my adult life from something I can only describe as My Sunday Sickness. This is what comes from listening intently during the sermon. Sleepers and the indifferent Awake are never afflicted, and that they are dead or indifferent to the preacher is no test of their faith: it could be a testament to their wisdom."[2] Clergymen as a rule adopt a tone of voice, a turn of phrase, a hollowness of the head which, in any other locale, would either bring people to their aid or have them winking behind their back. It is not clear that the faith of Christian congregations has suffered all that much from this messy-minded sort of worship. Possibly most of them have, either unwittingly or as a gesture of protection, suspended belief while at church. Or, worse yet, while at their prayers they are in the habit of shutting down those powers of mind and spirit where belief resides.

Humbuggery we shall always have with us, but there is, I submit, a still further cause of our present disaffection which may entail more snarled theology than atrocious performance. The objection one often hears is that worship is "ritual". "Ritual" is in this context a dirty word, a slur, like "ceremony", "rite", "formality", "observance". The implication is that even if intelligently and devoutly undertaken, it could not escape a certain intrinsic impotence. Not only for unbelievers, but especially for believers most energetically keyed to social service, liturgy is considered to be a romantic if dutiful dalliance, a solemnity of play, with enough bunk about it to be of little consequence. My purpose in discussing it further is not to inquire into how worship can go bad,

---

2"Short and Select," *The Commonweal*, August 5, 1949, p. 415.

leaving this to the ample evidence available to every reader. I would rather pursue the point that liturgy is of *highest* consequence precisely because it is ritual.

What, then, is ritual? It would include dramatic gestures of all sorts. The presentation of the Belgian ambassador to Queen Elizabeth II is a ritual. So was last autumn's Harvard-Yale football game. A presentation of Puccini's *Madama Butterfly* at La Scala opera house is a ritual. So also General De Gaulle's triumphal march through the boulevards of Paris the day after the Allies re-took the city. The American flag raised every day over an Akron tire factory is ritual. The awarding of medals at the conclusion of an international skiing competition is ritual, and so is the competition itself. Thomas and Marilyn's wedding last Saturday was ritual, as was its sexual consummation. President Kennedy's state funeral was ritual, and so were the gestures made at National Guardsmen by hostile Berkeley students during the strife over People's Park.

Ritual as Powerful

Rituals can be sources of surprising power. Several years ago, for example, when the Czech ice hockey team bested the Russians in an internationally televised match, Prague erupted with demonstrations. Czech citizens burned Russian flags, disgraced Soviet statues, and wrecked the Aeroflot booking office downtown. Both the game and the riotous outburst were only ritual, but they were the only avenue of defiance offered to a people who in every substantial way had been laid under brutal and humiliating subjection. About the same time, when Honduras reported a victory over El Salvador in (soccer) football, Salvadorian troops invaded their neighbor country and sat there in vengeful occupation until the defeat had been effaced. In Glasgow, where Protestant Scots and Catholic Irish work and dwell side-by-side in fierce hostility, the annual football match between the (Protestant) Rangers and (Catholic) Celtics is occasion for mayhem. The stadium is stoutly divided by the city's entire police force and coils of barbed wire; yet it is not uncommon for a hundred fans to be taken to the hospital with injuries. Some years back, a retired Protestant pensioner living in very low-cost municipal housing brought suit against the Glasgow city council because the door and wooden trim of his dwelling had been painted green. When judgment was given against him, rather than endure further offense to his religious sensibilities, he vacated the house and went to live in much more costly lodgings at his own expense. Back in 1936 Hitler so staged and managed the Olympic Games in Berlin that they served and glorified the Third Reich, and people who today remember those games still feel the keen resentment felt in all nations, and the sympathy felt in return for snubbed athletes like Jesse Owens.

The examples I have selected to typify the power that can be released by ritual are, as it happens, all drawn from sports. Since almost all athletic games are symbolic pantomimes of warfare, they can easily evoke and trigger the primitive forces of aggression that lie so close beneath the surface of sporting competition. Sports, however, offer but one example of a power common to all rituals. When they are called upon to transact through symbols the unstable and unresolved relations between people, they often buckle under the weight, and release explosive power. Thus ritual somehow can be made to serve false purposes. When symbol must replace substance, it eventually smolders and combusts.

Another thing about ritual: if it is performed improperly, if somehow it is at cross-purposes with itself, the impropriety can cause deep anguish and even anger. For instance, high offense is taken by some who read their newspapers and learn that marriage services are now being celebrated for homosexual couples in San Francisco churches. Objectors who brought more than emotion to bear might still object that such a deviant wedding concerns not simply two gay men who plan to live together, but that by publicly consecrating such an unstable union, it casts a cloud of confusion over all marriages. When an uncle has too much to drink and becomes argumentative at the family dinner on Christmas day, it is much more vexing than on any other occasion. Christmas dinner is meant to celebrate something quite other than what uncle is stridently doing. Then there was the marriage, back in 1969, of one of the late President Kennedy's better-known aides. *The New York Times* reported that the service was conducted in a local church described by the bride as "very liberal and denominationally like a Unitarian church, although that is not in its name." The minister "performed what he called 'a traditional service, but with some modifications, mainly the deletion of outmoded Christian phraseology.' " Since this was, as noted by the *Times*, the third lady this gentlemen had taken to wife, one could imagine a number of the traditional Christian phrases that would grate upon the ceremony, whereas the usual musical themes from *Lohengrin* and *A Midsummer Night's Dream* were reported to have blended smoothly into the service.

Ritual must be congruent. Why is it that we recoil when Napoleon crowns himself, when Jesus is betrayed by Judas with a kiss, when Scobey (in Graham Greene's *The End of the Affair*) receives communion sacrilegiously, when the Reverend Elmer Gantry seduces his lithesome female converts in the tall grass, when the Mafia chieftains are given Christian burial? Why is it that the King of the Ammonites, "Hanun seized David's servants, shaved off half of each man's beard, cut their clothes half way up to the buttocks, and sent them away"? (2 Samuel 10, 4). Why did a mob of construction workers in New York City storm City Hall and tear down the flag which had been flying at half-mast in sympathy for Kent State students killed by the National Guard? Why did Marines risk their lives to plant the flag on Mount Suribachi even before Iwo Jima was safely in their hands? Why must Oedipus tear his own eyes out after he learns he has slain his father and lain with his mother, all unawares? Why do parents invite their many friends to a party on their child's christening day? Why did Governor Lester Maddox refuse to attend Martin Luther King's funeral? What strange power does ritual have, that it must be, and it must be right?

Briefly, why must we have ritual in our lives? And why do we insist — vehemently at times — that it be fitting and harmonious to the occasion? Because it is through ritual that we bring purpose into our lives. Our rituals provide us with intense moments of meaning, opportunities to display the powerfully operative forces that shape the way we live. It is by ritual that we embody why we live and celebrate what we believe. Ritual releases meaning. Better put: it craves meaning, and can possess it only from other kinds of human activity. It cannot supply meaning, it only reveals it.

Sex: The Ritual of Marriage

Let sexual intercourse serve here as in instance of ritual. It is, by the nature of things, the oldest of human symbols, far more primitive even than speech. It is also powerful: powerful enough in the lives of individuals to fuel deep love and hate, powerful enough in the life of mankind to have given birth to the social institutions of marriage and family. Men and women can seek to convey in sex any number of relations. It can mean nothing: only a nonchalant exchange of orgasm. It can mean that a man and a woman are attracted by one another. Or that they love one another. Or that they rejoice in mutual fidelity. Or, in that further reach of meaning released by Christianity, that they rejoice in unconditional mutual fidelity, for better, for worse, for richer, for poorer, in sickness and in health, until death.

The conviction within the Christian tradition has been that, whatever purposes sex may be put to by men and women, it offers fulfilment only when it embodies perpetual fidelity. Not only does it give no rest otherwise; it corrupts, it deceives, it lures folk to destruction. This view collides most obviously with the popular conviction that sex embodies love. To contend against this view, one would observe that we have many man-woman loves in our lives that are of the most intimate kind, yet do not crave sexual exchange. Does a man love his mother the less because he declines to sleep with her? Or does love for his sisters and daughters somehow fall short of the mark for want of sex? What sex craves to embody is not simply, "I love you," but "I am one with you forever."

The symbolism of sexual intercourse is the surrender of privacy. A man and woman give their bodies in diverse ways to all their friends and loves, but they surrender their whole body, their "private parts" (as quaintly and rightly called), only to the partner with whom they share unqualified privacy. Children and parents may exchange the fullest love possible, yet their mutual need is that the children acquire their own privacy, and move off into healthy independence. Only with his wife does a man submerge his privacy and purposes and decision-making and home. Thus sex craves to embody and celebrate the mystery of a man and a woman who have surrendered their individual loves to one another for the sake of the deeper and more fruitful life they have in common. It is not just any sort of love, or just the most intense love, but the peculiarly dedicated type of love that unites as closely as humans can, and differently.

It is not sex, though, that draws husband and wife together. The actual business of two persons becoming one in love is the exchange of mutual service. A man loves his wife when he senses without being told that she has a headache, when he mows the lawn before it gets shaggy, cares for the runny noses of their children when he is with them, allows for her own growth in career, and wipes the ring out of the bathtub. It is not in bed that he makes love to his wife. He does that when he wipes the ring out of the tub. It is in bed that he celebrates the love that grows between them as he keeps wiping the ring out of the tub. And it is utterly urgent that he do have sex with his wife, that he celebrate the meaning the daily and mundane services have for them, that in their ritual they both release and impose the meaning that their adventure together has for them, lest it end disappointingly in being nothing more than wiping the ring out of the tub. What marriage and fidelity and two-in-one-flesh require is not only that a man wash the ring out of the tub, but that he grow together into one with his wife, in *love*. That love grows, not only from the services done, but from their having been done as services.

Thus two become one by bodily union. A husband and wife enjoy and foster two kinds of physical exchange: those that are substantial, and those that are symbolic. By mutual, bodily services they grow into loving persons; by joint rituals they ignite and fan the flame of love within those services. Thus ritual is verified by service, yet service is quickened by ritual. It is in sleeping with his wife that a man enjoys the ecstatic vision of what is at stake when he (excuse it again, but it *is* the point) washes the ring out of the tub. It is in washing the ring out of the tub that he becomes the loving man who can with full honesty sleep with his wife.

Ritual, then, is indeed never self-ratifying nor self-sufficient. It is the celebration that gives us insight into our lives, and drives us to live up to that insight. And it is not merely an expression of our beliefs and values. Like ethical activity, it works both from the inside out, and from the outside in. It expresses what lies within us, but it also shapes us in return. Of every true ritual it can be said (as Catholics have described sacraments): it effects what it signifies provided that what it signifies is already in effect. Where ritual is not ratified by service, there we have hypocrisy, sham, and magic. Where service is not given meaning by ritual, there we have drift and drudgery and an end of human civilization.

I take it that in our day we are well enough warned against the hypocrisy that comes from rituals unratified by service. But it would be no waste of effort to explore the opposite menace: that aimlessness and drift which follow from ritual that is distorted or frivolous or absent altogether. Ethical performance may be haphazard and distracted, or it may be purposeful. It is often ritual that makes the difference, by investing what we do with an inwardness that allows it to build us up, rather than simply to be an ephemeral event that leaves us ungrown.

Rituals of War and Peace

As illustrations of the sense and mettle of ritual, I should like to draw upon some events in the autumn of 1969 which, although they took place within the confines of university life, were so publicly reported as to be familiar even to the reader at large. I refer to the moratorium days at campuses across the country on October 15, and one month later in Washington.

On October 15, classes at Notre Dame were suspended for one day in favor of consideration of war and peace by the community. During the morning thousands of students, faculty, wives, and administrators gathered upon the main mall to hear all speak who would, upon the Vietnamese war. Radicals spoke; an ex-marine returned from combat spoke for the war and was cheered; time was given to a tailor from town who had escaped Hungary in 1956 (he had been a Freedom Fighter in those other, forgotten, October days). It was a brisk autumn day, but there was a hush upon the crowd that was curiously reverent. Near mid-day all present rose and were deftly convoyed by marshals into a long parade, six abreast, some with arms linked. At intervals down the length of the line men carried large wooden crosses aloft, reminiscent of Holy Week ceremonies in Seville. Between the crosses, sharing the sky, large banners unfurled: the banners were black, without words. So too, was the procession, which walked the length of the mall in grave silence.

The marchers (or pilgrims?) regrouped beside the ROTC building, where the campus units of the armed services are quartered. Across from the main entrance they then planted in the soil nine white crosses, one by one, as for graves of nine Notre Dame graduates who had been killed in the Vietnamese conflict. Nine times a bugler sounded taps.

Then once again the cluster regrouped itself, six abreast, to file back the full length of the campus. Only this time the banners had been reversed, and although they still spoke with no words, they were bright scarlet. The marchers sang together with one voice for the entire walk. Then, gathered under an enormous mural of Christ with arms upraised, all entered into a celebration of the Eucharist, led by an archbishop from India whose work for peace and political amnesty had gained him a name for courage. At the offertory a group of seven alumni, teachers, and students presented their draft registration cards which a young female student destroyed before the altar.

My point in recounting the story is not to solicit sympathy for the aims of the day, but to point out how young people who were presumed to be hostile towards ritual (and who, if asked, would probably say it was so) spontaneously fell back upon the most primitive symbols to embody their resistance to the war. The rituals struck home. As I drove by the nine funereal crosses later that day, I was stopped by the discovery that was something more than mere reminder: I had known three of the nine boys personally. It was important, too, that the bugler sound the full melody of Taps nine times over — to din it into the souls of all present that men had died nine times over. Everyone present *knew* about the war, and already had convictions of all sorts about it. But the ritual made one shiver in his bones.

That same day, deep in the prairies of Kansas a gathering of anti-war demonstrators marched for thirty miles, from town to town. The story was told me by an elderly woman, wife of a Russian who had fled the Bolsheviks and his homeland nearly fifty years earlier, and had brought his Swiss wife to find and cherish freedom in being American. They and many of their fellow-marchers were Mennonites, devoted pacifists, many of whom had been imprisoned or maltreated for their beliefs during World War II. Feeling still runs sharp against them in that part of Kansas. As they walked along, the lady told me, the road was lined to right and left with onlookers, most of them antagonistic, and many of them waving, or rather brandishing, small American flags at the silent demonstrators. She noticed that the same faces would re-appear: evidently the onlookers themselves were running forward from place to place to re-demonstrate against the demonstrators. It was all she could do, she confessed, to keep from asking for one of the taunting flags, so that she could hold it before her: the flag she had come across continent and ocean to make her own.

As they trudged along, an enormous bell was borne on a wagon, to toll once for each American dead in the war. When it struck, she said, she imagined some young man, with a mother and family and an emptiness of grief left behind. It took but a few seconds for the echoes to reverberate away across the prairie, and then it tolled again, and again, and relentlessly again. "Each time", she said, "it struck my heart: *another* boy, *another* family, and perhaps a young wife and little ones." Here again, the ritual had its effect. Those who grieved for the war, and those who called for loyalty to it, both found their hearts rising within them as they marched to the clash of symbols. And as for the bell: everyone there *knew* that there had been 38,000 American dead, but somehow it pierced the heart when the bell struck so many, many times.

One month later, November 15, countless thousands gathered in Washington to renew the protest. In one of the most poignant rituals of the day, 38,000 people were given large placards bearing the name and home state of one of the fallen. Slowly they filed across the federal grounds, up to the esplanade before the White House, where each marcher laid his memorial card in an open coffin. The rite was simple, yet one girl recounted that as she stood in the somber mortuary line for long, slowpaced hours, the name in her hands slowly came to life, as a very personal boy from some town in Illinois. The longer she held him the more he quickened, until the grieving moment when she had to let him go to his death—in the coffin. Briefly the ritual had touched her at the quick: she had seen a young man die; the war had disclosed in a flash its horror.

Regardless of one's stance on the terribly complex misery of the war in Viet Nam, one can see in these hastily composed folk rituals the power that they had to embody belief, to expose conscience in a new and effectual way to the pathos of so many distant and anonymous deaths. The repeated wailing of the bugle, the relentless tolling of the bell of the dead, the long walk with a dead boy's name in one's arms—all these dinned into good citizens what it was that their nation was doing. Like Hamlet, they fell to drama, hoping the play would be the thing whereby to catch the conscience of the king. . .and of themselves.

One is reminded of King David, who had gotten the wife of one of his mercenary officers pregnant. Trying to conceal his misadventure, he quickly arranges to have the man furloughed, but though the soldier is a Gentile, he stubbornly abides by the Jewish rule that in time of battle warriors were not to sleep with their wives. In his fury, the king has him posted to the most vulnerable spot in the front lines, and he is slain, leaving David free to take his wife for himself. Nathan, bolder than the ordinary run of court chaplains, confronts David with his own ritual, the ballad:

"In the same town were two men,
   one rich, the other poor.

The rich man had flocks and herds
in great abundance;
the poor man had nothing but a ewe lamb,
one only, a small one he had bought.
This he fed, and it grew up with him and his children,
eating his bread, drinking from his cup,
sleeping on his breast; it was like a daughter to him.
When there came a traveller to stay, the rich man
refused to take one of his own flock or herd
to provide for the wayfarer who had come to him.
Instead he took the poor man's lamb
and prepared it for his guest."

David's anger flared up against the man. "As Yahweh lives," he said to Nathan "the man who did this deserves to die! He must make fourfold restitution for the lamb, for doing such a thing and showing no compassion."

Then Nathan said to David, "You are the man." (2 Samuel 12, 1-7)

We are all somewhat strangers to our own hearts. It is for ritual to disclose to us these deep springs within us, so that we can ever re-reckon the worth of the work of our hands.

Worship: Rituals of Belief

Now, then, we can turn to that particular form of ritual which embodies our beliefs about how we stand before God: worship. Christians understand their own particular traditions of worship by reference to Jesus Christ, whose entire life is characterized by the gospels as a ritual. Jesus is himself a sacrament, the benevolence of the Father fleshed among men. In his manhood he reveals God: incompletely, tantalizingly, invitingly. As he passes from village to village, he feeds the hungry, raises the dead, fraternizes with the whores and traitors, heals the paralyzed and the sickly, washes away the sins of those who repent. His every act is a ritual: the incarnation discloses the Father, not simply in the words of the Son, but in his every gesture and service. Nevertheless, though it is through the touch of his body that he reveals the love of the Father and conveys his life, he makes flesh—his and ours—the conveyance of more inward gifts than flesh could receive. To believe in Jesus is to see that there is more to him than meets the eye: that he who is man is more than man. Just so: to believe in his sacramental rituals is to see that there is more to sharing among men than meets the eye: that all service of neighbor is more than human service.

Let the Eucharist be a case in point. The ritual of the Eucharist is that of a meal. Any disciple emerging from the Last Supper could have explained right out that he had been to a meal. It was no ordinary meal, because commemorative of Jewish liberation, but it was, with all its special prayers and observances, a meal. Unfortunately, most Christian worshippers issuing forth from the Eucharist on Sunday morning would have no such clear understanding of what they had just shared in. Still: it is a sacred supper. At the head of the table stands one who stands for Christ. He shares among his fellows hallowed bread and wine. What binds this brotherhood together is a common belief that in Jesus is embodied the Father, the creator of men. They further believe that whenever any man shares the substance of life with his brother, more passes between them than simple food, or nourishment, or the goods of the body. Just as what appear to be but bread and wine are by their profound inwardness become the conveyances of the body and blood of Jesus crucified and risen; thus these believers celebrate their belief that whenever they give generously to their neighbors, their gifts are but tokens of their own flesh and blood, and in turn tokens of the flesh and blood, the divine life, of the Son himself.

Sacraments are a celebration of faith. They are not the events by which we are rescued, and emerge from our sins, and are transformed into loving men. This we do by the daily exchanges of life with our brothers. In fact, worship is an interlude in the actual business of salvation. It deals in symbol, not in substance. In the Eucharist no concrete, substantial sharing of bread, and of all the supports of life that bread represents, is given from man to man. What is shared is a token bread. And it is only in the real order of work and sacrifice that men are transformed. Yet this interlude is a most necessary one. It is the pause we need to glimpse the inwardness and the purpose and the eternal worth of what we do when we work.

I suggested earlier that between husband and wife, sexual union is an interlude in the real business of love, a pause in the tempering and annealing service that smelts the two into one flesh. Yet it is in sex that they rediscover and refresh their belief that these costly services are tokens of something even more precious. So in the Eucharist. It is not in church that we make love, that we are saved, that we emerge from selfishness into charity. Church is the one place in the world where one does not work out one's salvation. The sanctuary is not the place set aside for us to encounter God (whom we are unremittingly reminded to seek in our neighbor), but the sacred place where we draw aside momentarily to rediscover and refresh our faith that it is in serving our neighbor that we cleave to God.

It is entirely appropriate that Christians would eventually devise the custom of dedicating a recurring day to leisure. They have their own compelling reasons for valuing work and service, and further reasons for needing time free to draw back from the work. For without worship gifts passed from hand to hand can cease to be gifts, and are in danger of degenerating into nothing more than commercial trans-

actions. A token is a token only so long as the giver sees it as
a conveyance of something he cannot hold within his hand.
The Eucharist, a leisureful celebration, is the secret of those
who believe that man cannot live by bread alone, yet by the
gift of bread they can and do receive more than bread alone.

One peculiarity of Christian rituals is that their customary form is not that of a prayer service: a cluster of
worshippers gathered in an attentive attitude to address God
and be obedient to his commands. The gathering is focused,
not upon an absent God, but rather upon the minister, the
man who stands in place of Christ. The ritual activity is not
addressed to God so much as to man: the minister sacrament-
ally continues the work of Jesus, who healed, nourished,
fraternized, forgave. To understand what the priest is
ordained to do we must not ask what it is he can do that
other believers cannot. For the very purpose of his celebra-
tory ritual is to display before all his fellows in sacramental
symbol the resonance, the similarity, the common power that
invests the work of Jesus and their work. The sacrament is
the thing by which he catches the conscience of his
congregation, revealing to them that in their everyday,
secular, humane occupations, eternity is at stake.

A church's rituals are the most peculiar possessions it
has. Apart from its ordained ministers, who are in any case
commissioned to preside at worship, sacramental rituals are
about the only other things which belong specifically to the
churches, which have no meaning or existence outside their
walls. Of them can be said all that I put forth earlier about
Christ and about the Church. The specific purpose of worship
is not to save, but to reveal that there is a God who is at all
times saving. Sacraments are not meant to draw one's
attention away from his secular pursuits, as from a distraction. On the contrary, what they celebrate is the salvific
power of common activities performed with uncommon
generosity. One draws away from one's work to contemplate
it, rather than to forget it. Liturgy does not afford a man an

occasion of retreat, so that he may step aside momentarily and attend to his intimacy with God which is neglected during those workaday times when he is preoccupied with matters mundane. It was never intended as a refuge from the mundane. It does not offer access to the Father any more immediate than one has elsewhere. Nor does it offer a forum wherein one may remedy his faults and shed his sins. Worship reveals one's Lord to man, and also reveals his own heart to him. It offers no escape from the world, but casts over it the high-intensity brilliance of faith.

The Minister: Handler of Rituals

This raises an important issue regarding the ministers, or priests, who celebrate these sacred rituals. Most religious functionaries earn their bread "by the gospel". They are freed from absorbing secular occupations, to be untrammeled in the service of their fellow believers. But this creates a problem. The priest must ever be bringing to his neighbors the symbols of service, but rarely the substance. This does not absolutely disqualify him, but it surely makes it difficult. How can one preside with effectiveness and grace at the Eucharist, gathering men around the table to break for them the bread of Jesus Christ, when one is not in any way accustomed to sharing the hospitality of his own table with friends and strangers? If the priest himself is to be a sacrament, and the role of host and householder is foreign to him, he must falter in his attempts to embody Jesus' welcome at the head of the table.

Another example might be the anointing of the sick. When men lie ill—particularly when the illness leads towards death—their entire person ails. Pain and misery and fear can infect the spirit as well as the flesh, and a man can become increasingly drawn into himself, anxious only for his own relief and comfort. In the gospel Jesus turns especial affection towards the sick and crippled, not only because in succoring them he could most publicly reveal the lifegiving love of the Father, but because these folk above all were tempted by dread and misfortune to look after themselves alone. The healing he gives penetrates all the way to the heart. Those he restores are instructed to sin no more, and are sent on their way to turn their energies towards others. I recall being struck one day at Lourdes, when I realized that on those holy grounds there were innumerable healings, far more healings than cures. Men and women of cold and fretful spirit were blessed and made whole. It was embodied for me when I saw a woman in a wheelchair being pushed by a man with a wooden leg. Now how can a man come to the bedside of a person sick unto death, and anoint him with the healing oil of the church, if this is the only way he participates in the healing process? How can he celebrate their common belief that whenever one person nurses another in his weakness, he brings him healing of spirit as well as of body, he reconciles him to the Father? Much better to confide this ministry to some of the weathered and gentle nurses who have more bedside manner, because they have incorporated the gift of healing into their persons.

I do not mean to suggest that a person has to exercise the full range of human services to qualify as a minister or priest. I would urge, though, that if a man of religion have no work of his own except the ministry of symbols, he will likely lack the power to make them reveal much. The celebrant should earn his bread by rendering some form of costly service that will enable him to take the symbols of Jesus' succoring into his hands and have a true feel for them. [3]

---

[3]There is the further problem that if a clergyman is paid by the very persons he must preach to, the gospel is likely to be softened lest he give offense.

In this chapter I have been pleading that worship is no replacement for ethics. They do, though, conspire together. Ethics ratifies worship, and worship in turn illumines ethics. Men find their motivation and insight in worship, they return to their work with redoubled generosity and conviction. And the resonance between their worship and work makes all genuine service of others revealing. Symbol gains substance; substance becomes symbolic of something deeper still. The word becomes flesh; flesh begins to speak.[4]

It would seem terribly difficult to speak with the raw strength of the gospel to those who have one on the payroll. In the Old Testament, the better prophets generally tended to be those who were not beholden to the king, and thus had nothing to lose when rebuking him. In our own time, Abbé Pierre comments: "One no longer dares to preach the fullness of the Gospel in churches because the faithful manages to pamper the clergy so much that priests can no longer preach the true Gospel without being embarrassed. This is a very sound collective ruse which places the clergy in a bourgeois state which neither the Lord nor His Apostles knew. Thus, it is pretty sure that certain pages of the Gospel will be preached no longer. . .*To remain free,* the prophet must have a work which will assure his complete economic independence, be it the lowest—like rag-picking at Emmaus—so that he may stand sovereign in his liberty." "A Prophet in America," *Jubilee* III, 2 (June, 1955), 11 & 13.

[4]See the very fine chapter, "Ethics as Language," in Herbert McCabe's *What is Ethics All About?* (Washington: Corpus, 1969), pp. 68-103.

6 The Prodigal Father, and How His Sons Draw Close to Him

To illustrate the last chapter's insight, I should like to dwell first upon Penance, and then upon prayer.

Penance

There is a double reason for selecting the sacrament of Penance as a ritual to be considered. To begin with, it is timely. During the last decade of revival in the Catholic Church, one practice that has eluded all revival is confession. Indeed, it has undergone an abrupt decline. There has been no public campaign against confession, no dissuasion in the press, no bitter complaint. But by an almost spooky simultaneity, most Catholics in North America and Northern Europe have either indefinitely postponed or stopped it altogether. The scent of sulphur puckers the nostrils much less in church nowadays, and apparently when people feel less constrained than they once did, they leave off going to this sacrament. It may have won less affection from the faithful than even we used to believe when reading pamphlets that chided the Protestants for doing away with this necessary sacrament.

An inquiry into Penance, though, is even more timely on a larger calendar. It has for centuries suffered some confusion. The documents of the New Testament suggest that deadly sin after Baptism was not then seriously contemplated, and no provision for subsequent re-conversion was made. Only in the fourth century, when recent defectors from the North African church wanted to return after persecutions, was it finally understood that one might fall despite Baptism, and need to be forgiven and restored. Penance, the celebration of the sinners' return, was known as "the second plank after shipwreck". For long centuries it was resorted to only for the three major crimes of adultery, apostasy, and murder. The emphasis was upon *penance:* a stringent discipline to be undergone, not so much for communal vengeance or public humiliation or as a warning to others, but to purge out the evil passions that had gained the mastery in the sinner's heart. One had sinned; now one had to unlive the sin. In a later age, when Christians fastened their fascination less upon God and more upon the Church, emphasis in the sacrament swerved towards *reconciliation.* One was on the outs with the community and sought readmission. Churchmen replaced the ancient forms of restorative penance with rituals: prayers, pilgrimages to shrines, enlistment in the crusades, etc. A third period ensued, during which the scope of sin became vastly enlarged. Penance was enjoined, not only for public crimes, but for the numberless infringements of the alarmingly lengthy catalogue of commandments published by preachers. Now the emphasis shifted to *confession.* One had to tell all.

The sacrament has thus detached itself from the process of ethical transformation, and in the popular mind offers itself precisely as a substitute for what was primitively understood as penance. Penance was originally an energetic and painstaking refashioning of a misused man. Now it has become an instant cure, a magic rite. It may be that the present disaffection among Catholics is a reaction to the inadequacies that led Protestants to abandon the custom and Orthodox to neglect it. Thus an investigation might be timely, particularly in this season of search for ecumenical unity.

The other reason for me to venture these remarks is that I can find no other single point across the entire field of Christian thought and practice where more misunderstandings converge. The sacrament of Penance, as preached, practiced, and understood, is afflicted by every one of the distortions that this book is at pains to identify and relieve.

To begin with, most folk come to confession with the idea that it is God whom it will change, rather than themselves. The penitent approaches God to solicit his forgiveness. He presents himself, and once he has admitted his guilt and pleaded his sincerity, the words of forgiveness are offered, from the confessor and from the God whom he represents. If anyone undergoes ethical transformation, it is the Father. The idea is that he withholds forgiveness until the sinner has sought and deserved it. First the sinner repents; then God forgives. But this is all a denial of what Jesus discloses about his Father: that he *is* Forgiveness, that reconciliation between ourselves and him requires no change in him, but a healing in ourselves that his extravagant love might finally penetrate us. Reconciliation does not involve our seeking him, or our placating him. He must seek *us* out.

It is commonly understood that initiative in this sacrament rests with the penitent. The gospel, I submit, has it all the other way around. Jesus is not approached by persons seeking forgiveness. He offers it, urges it upon his hearers, always makes the approach to them. This is nowhere expressed better than in the parable of the Prodigal Son in Luke 15. Actually the tale is misnamed: it is the father in the story who is prodigal. Little is said of the son save that he stalks out of home and family and loses his share of the family fortune (the proceeds of his father's land and toil) in circumstances suggestive of Tijuana or Port Said. Ruined and desperate, he heads home again in hope of at least a job and a full belly. The story never suggests that he has a change of heart; it is still the same Schlemiel of a son who comes up the road. But the father has been waiting. He does not let the son walk up to the door, but runs to meet him. He does not permit him to finish his prepared job-hunting speech, but sweeps him into his arms and commands a household celebration. If that were not enough, the story then continues to describe the outrage of the older brother, whose sense of justice provides even sharper contrast with the spend-thrift affection of the father.

As things now stand, the pentitent is summoned to submit himself, to humiliate himself for his misdeeds before priest and Lord. But in the parable, if anyone humiliates himself it is the father, who throws himself without guile upon the hearts of his sons. They may either rebuke him for being a fool, or be overwhelmed by his love and respond with like sincerity. The man who would be deputized for Christ has no business summoning his weak and sordid brothers before him to be forgiven. He must at his own risk offer his open affection to them in their offenses, and draw them into forgiveness. His task is not to sit ready to administer the protocols of reconciliation to those who have already come to terms with their failures, but to reach out and touch and heal those who had not given it much thought before his arrival. The initiative in the sacrament, then, must lie with the minister, and he must represent a God who in no way will alter his love for the sinner through this sacrament. He will not relent, cannot be placated, demands no atonement: because, like his deputy, though better, he does not turn away in disdain in the first place.

Another feature of Penance that has been twisted wrong way round is that of revelation. By rights a sacrament, like Jesus himself, should bring beneficial disclosure to a believer: a disclosure of his own character and of the Father's. But in confession all disclosure has been by the penitent. Nothing is discovered; he comes precisely to tell what he already knows. The minister has nothing to reveal. And such disclosure as there is leaves no one much the better for it. Certainly the confessor does not come away much the wiser man, nor is that the purpose of the exchange.

The structure of the sacrament has been turned into something reminiscent of a tribunal. The priest sits in judgment on the misadventures of the penitent, and assigns a token penalty. It is a thorough embodiment of the forensic metaphor I discussed in Chapter III. And a grotesque confusion. For the one thing a judge can never do is to forgive. He can condemn or acquit, but never forgive. And the one thing Jesus does not do on behalf of the Father is to punish. The dynamics of a criminal court are perhaps least apt to serve as an embodiment of what God is trying to do in his forgiveness.

Sin

The sacrament reaches deeply into beliefs about ethics, and here it institutionalizes some of the worst misunderstandings about sin. For example, the catechism recounts that a serious sin, one which would separate a person from amity with God and destroy all graced love in his heart, has three distinct requirements: grievous matter, sufficient reflection, and full consent. Surely there could be no more misleading description of sin.

There is a whelming amount of sin in life, but remarkably little "grievous matter". Most of the sordidness and selfish neglect takes less spectacular forms than grand larceny, aggravated assault or perjury. As Rose Macaulay put it so vividly, sin begins with the puny thieveries of a child, and need not clothe itself in grotesque form to have eaten out a man's heart. As for sufficient reflection, it is the last thing we enjoy when messing in evil. A clear head and an open eye are precisely what we shun. When bent upon our own self-aggrandizing purposes, we confuse ourselves with double-talk of the mind, we emit a cloud of "if's" and "but's", we never look ourselves in the eye. Evil is hardly reflective. We manage to harbor within us far more sin than malice. And as for full consent: no one ever fully consents to evil. We always sidle into it, we back up to the edge of the cliff and wait for the wind to come. We speak of our embarrassments as "having happened to us", or simply as "having happened".

In a word, we search for responsibility as the hallmark of sin, whereas the serious selfishness in our lives is furtive. A penitent asks himself what he has done that is monstrously evil, contemplated soberly, and then deliberately committed — with the intention of flinging affront to God. Since he has not assassinated an archbishop lately, he may reckon that there is not much by way of serious sin to apologize for.

The particulars and customs that invest confession each add their own frustrations. For example, the confessional itself seems designed only to thwart the purposes of the sacrament. If the minister is to embody the forgiveness of the Father, not simply in his words, but with his entire person, then the thorough-going personal exchange that is wanted can hardly be helped by the closeted secrecy and anonymity of the confessional. It is argued that the very sordid character of men's offenses leads them to prefer anonymity. But the point of a sacrament is that a man is sent to embody the Father as Jesus embodied him, and one is opened to the Father's forgiveness only insofar as he is actually exposed to the person of his minister: not his words through the wall, but his person.

Then there has been the generally approved custom of very frequent confession. This has encouraged a trivializing of sin. No person can scrutinize his life in serious depth if he is doing it every few weeks. If one does try to give an account of himself too often, he begins to talk about surface odds-and-ends instead of overall trends or significant behavior. The Church has encouraged this too by calling for very specific lists of sins and information as to frequency and circumstances. What emerges is not a report from the conscience, but a journalistic account of utter superficiality: no insight, no conviction, just a routine report: dutiful but impotent.

There is the further custom of making one's confession to absolutely any priest available. I am certainly not urging that every priest must be as devout and shrewd as Philip Neri or Father Zosima (in *The Brothers Karamazov*) before one dare open one's conscience to him. But the sacrament makes great demands upon its minister. If it is simply a perfunctory exchange, wherein a penitent recites in adequate detail the particulars of his sins, and a priest responds in an equally routine way the formula for absolution, then ordination is surely the only requisite. But if a man is to reach into the heart of another with the forceful candor and delicate gentleness of Jesus Christ, then it is a highly personal task, and calls for a man of sensitivity, honesty, savvy, and compassion. Quite frankly, these are qualities that do not abound in wasteful profusion among our clergy. Perhaps that is to be expected in a church which deliberately deprives itself of good ministers by ordaining only those who are willing to forego marriage, rather than choosing those men who have already displayed those graces one looks for in a man of God. In any case, the custom has too often been to bring one's sins to the nearest priest available, or to the least inquisitive.

Here I should like to enter a word of scepticism about a rather new custom that is increasingly attractive: the practice of general absolution. Good priests rightly distressed at the sight of honest folk in their congregations hanging back from communion, yet loth to come to the confessional, have seized the expedient of offering everyone in church general absolution, on the express but not enforced condition that

those with sins on their consciences should submit them to
confession at some early occasion. If one is content simply to
augment the headcount at communion, this will serve. But
meanwhile it reinforces all those vexatious misunderstandings
that spook the people away from confession. First, they are
confirmed in their belief that many are in mortal sin, banned
from communion, for having missed Mass on Sunday or
masturbated or (in yesteryear) eaten meat on Friday.
Meanwhile the weightier matters of human conduct, those
more massive but painless ills of the soul, go all unnoticed.
Second, one continues to believe that release from sin is done
in the waving of a hand and the invocation of words. Trivial
sin; trivial repentance. And the community continues on,
ignorant of that intimate sacramental encounter wherein one
man learns joyfully to share his conscience with another.
They are led to prefer mass meetings where any skitterish
conscience can be easily lost in the crowd.

I have spoken all to one side of the issue, putting the
finger on the feeble and faltering features of the sacrament of
Penance as conventionally understood and practiced. Many
devout and shrewd priests today sit in forgiveness, and many
believers find new depth to their sincerity and compunction
in the confessional. But for the most part the rapid
disaffection across whole fields of the Church which had
previously been known as peculiarly attached to this
sacrament — this disaffection only shows that faithful Christians never did sense the gift given in Penance. For many who
have given themselves faithfully and regularly to confession,
no great discovery has been the reward, because the
sacrament has been misconstrued and misministered. As one
young Englishman once wrote me: "But now I am
astounded by the possibility for sin, by my personal
uselessness; how can I express all that I know is wrong in me?
My incapability to express this results in my 'shopping list'
confession, my reeling off of a series of 'sins' purely symbolic

of the inner wrong I feel. But is my duty done? My confession has on the one hand satisfied the basic requirements of my religious scruples and yet my ego is still intact!"

A Burden to Conscience, not a Relief

The gospel speaks often of forgiving, but perhaps the most fetching tale is that of Zacchaeus. He is a tiny man, but important: he holds high rank amoung the publicans who act as agents for the occupying Roman authorities to tax their fellow Jews. Publicans were understandably pariahs among their own countrymen, and also not noted for their honesty. One day Zacchaeus wanders over to see the hubbub when Jesus comes to town. To his surprise, the prophet singles him out of the crowd and invites himself to lunch and lodge at his house. In the midst of his entertainment the publican blurts out to his guest that he is giving away half of his fortune to the poor, and making over fourfold damages to those he had defrauded. At the close of the story Jesus only observes that this is why he prefers to seek out the company of sinners.

In the story, Zacchaeus only approaches Jesus with common curiosity; it is Jesus who asks for companionship. There are no reproaches, no accusations, not even innuendos. It is simply the presence of this overwhelmingly simple and honest man that gets to Zacchaeus, who had spent his wit and work on gouging his townsmen. Jesus comes to his home and leaves a transformed man behind.

The Church's service of forgiving must ever be the same. Men of profound and singlehearted affection and service must speak out the simple call of Jesus, and must ask for the companionship of every one they pass, most particularly the most offensive or inert. Those whom they touch to the heart will accept their readiness to be invited into their consciences. In this intimate encounter, men will not come to priests to help them be freed from what perturbs their consciences. This would be an easy task, and also a less fruitful one. What they must do is ask the priests to help them discover what never gets on their consciences.

The revelation in Penance is twofold. A man calls on another to help him search his heart with comradely honesty. Together they discover the furtive sins, the crafty and familiar selfishness, the offenses that are unforgiven because unsuspected, unrepented, unforsworn. On the other side of the exchange, the priest reveals to the penitent that in the face of his pettiness and fault, he loves him all the same, he loves him all the more. And so he embodies the love of the Father and of the Son, who cherish men in their deepest misery. As in all sacraments there is the twofold discovery: God's grace and man's sin. And the two are most meshingly intertwined. A man opens his heart and allows himself to discover fault never earlier acknowledged, precisely because he is in the company of one whom he trusts will not hold him in contempt. And the love of the Father comes across to him with fullest force precisely because it is incarnated in one who knows his weakest self, yet embraces him as friend.

Thus confession is no apology to the Lord for acknowledged failure, and the comforting response that one's sin is set aside. The deputy of the Lord approaches one in the first place to help him find sin, and conveys to his frail brother that the Lord ever loves him no matter what his faults. The forgiveness is always there, but it is in this encounter, discovery, and purgation that it penetrates the bones of the man who needs it.

Penance is by no means the only means of forgiveness. God has but a single attitude towards man: he forgives. Better: he is Forgiveness. And reconciliation takes place whenever a man withdraws from his stubborn and blinded selfishness, to emerge into generosity and adulthood. This need involve no religion, no revelation. Man is forgiven as he is transformed into one who loves. It can be done with the help of anyone with candor and care. What the sacrament does is to enhance this transformation with the disclosure of how much is at stake. As one man speaks to another the words of absolution and forgiveness that Jesus Christ charges him to say, he reveals to his brother that *whenever* he ceases ignoring and exploiting his fellows, his brothers, he is thus being restored to his Father. In all aloofness from one's brother, one holds back from the Father. So too, whenever any man turns afresh towards his brothers, he thereby — whether he knows it or not — cleaves closer to the Father. Any moment that a man takes new counsel with himself or another and breaks through some trammeling of his ego, forgiveness comes to him. What is peculiar to sacramental reconciliation is that it brings faith to bear: one celebrates how eternally it matters that a man embrother his neighbor.

Penance and Eucharist call one another forth. In both, the summons of Jesus Christ is uttered: publicly in one, privately in the other. In the one, a spokesman puts the challenge to all men how they are loved and how they *ought* to live. At Eucharist one man embodies Christ to the community of believers. At Penance he singles men out one by one and pursues them to their consciences. Eucharist is the invitation to Penance. Penance is the threshing floor where grain and husk are beaten apart, where we are protected from being those who merely refrain, "Lord, Lord!" at Eucharist.

Guilt and Shame

One often hears that the purpose of confession is to relieve guilt. Yet in the gospel story, Zacchaeus approaches Jesus without any particular guilt; only when he draws close does he find himself beset by guilt on every side. The sacrament is gifted to us in order that we may discover sin, and incur guilt. The Church has insisted that guilt is a gift, not a discouragement. It is particularly so in the sacrament, where one simultaneously discovers the support of his Lord and of his brother.

Here I should like to introduce some remarks about guilt. C. G. Jung has spoken very favorably of the practice of confession. He had almost no psychiatric patients who were practicing Catholics, and explained that they had their pathological guilt feelings relieved in the confessional. Many practitioners of psychology and psychiatry feel differently, though, and accuse the church of worrying people into unnatural seizures of scruples and guilt. Perhaps this criss-cross of attitude arises from a confusion between what I should like to distinguish as shame and guilt.

Shame is a fear of the contempt of others. It arises from one's own misbehavior. The weaknesses need not really be public knowledge, for there is always the fear that they will be exposed, a brooding uneasiness that others might see through one. It surges up most often from the coupled sources of sex and violence. Misadventures of these kinds, after all, arise from passion; one feels curiously as if he had been "beside himself", and is anxious to disclaim his failure since he was not his real self. These are also the faults that we are most reluctant to publish. Craving for privacy is commonly known in the area of sex. Our recent self-condemnation for the war in Southeast Asia may give us fresh insights into the working of shame regarding the brutality of war. In any case, there are things we loathe ourselves for, and since we hunger mightily for the approval of others, we are shamed for them to know of what we have done. This is not guilt. It is akin to what Iris Murdoch describes: "Brooding about the past is so often fantasy of how one might have won and resentment that one didn't. It is that resentment which one so often mistakes for repentance."[1]

Those who care for us try to take the edge off shame by reassurance. They put it forward either that what we do is

---

[1]*Bruno's Dream* (New York: Dell, 1969), p. 163.

not so contemptuous, or that they and others commonly fall
into the same sewer. This kind of acceptance can be very
welcome, especially if one is in a mighty hunger for it. One is
relieved to be able to unburden to another, and suffer no
disdain. But this does nothing for guilt, and I doubt that the
alleviation of shame by itself is of much service in the deeps
of the heart. Today one hears passionate ballyhoo for the
various devices of instant intimacy — sensitivity sessions,
pentecostal prayer groups, and marathon group therapy on
the California seashore — which beguile anxious folk into
thinking they have found reassurance for their lives in a hasty
48 hours or a week. Actually, forced and artificial reassur-
ance-sessions of this sort can trigger explosions of the very
same sex and violence that festered beneath the shame they
aim to relieve. Relief of shame is a worthwhile endeavor, but
I doubt it can be done without resolution of the deeper
problems of guilt.

Christianity itself should contribute to the resolution of
shame, for it believes in a Father before whom there can be
no disgrace. He can have no contempt for us, since our
infamies are nothing in his eyes. Yet churchmen have ever
been tempted to use people's native shame to maneuver into
a position of advantage with them. The Lord whose
cherishing should be our greatest source of peace is again and
again disfigured by morbid preachers who prefer a god of
wrath.

Now guilt is a very different kind of dismay. In guilt one
is not so much afraid of being despised, as regretful that one
has damaged his neighbor by being self-serving, and sorrowful
that oneself has been so impervious to his needs. When I am
ashamed I dread that others may be unloving; when I am
guilty, I discover that it is I who am wanting in love. My
shame makes me worry what my neighbor will feel, whereas
my guilt fastens on his loss from my neglect. It is a more
substantive concern.

At first sight shame appears easier lifted than guilt, for

my neighbor can easily assure me of his acceptance, if he will, whereas the real personal harm that guilt sorrows over is not put aside by cheerful words. First appearances deceive; it is actually the other way around. The kindling of shame is the beginning of a trouble that can be endless. But guilt never really arises in a man's heart unless he is approaching the point of purging his fault. Guilt leads a man to determinations, to repentance, to unliving his pettiness. Thus the very onset of guilt is a moment of relief. We try to brush away shame by distracting ourselves; guilt fastens the eye firmly on fact. Shame we try to efface by a change of attitude; guilt, by a change of life. Guilt is never sublimated, for it need not be.

And it is the grace of the church to give men guilt, to open their eyes to themselves, to tell them the things their best friends should be telling them but won't. It invites men to confess their sins at the very moment of turning away from them. It urges no embarrassment on man in his misery, for it also reveals to him, through the resolute affection of the churchmen themselves, that unflinching love of the Father who cannot despise. Not only does the church seek to bring men guilt; it magnifies guilt, by revealing that to exploit one's brother is not simply a misfortune between man and man, but a foolish flight from God himself.

The King of Israel called Elijah the prophet "My enemy, the Troubler of Israel". The man who accepts to be sent as preacher, confessor, and friend must be a troubler. Yet when he stings the conscience it is consoling, not embarrassing. What a man he must be. He must be so clear of conscience that he can reveal to men the secrets of their own, without hedging to keep from playing the hypocrite. Blunt and candid he must be, the sort of friend who cannot conceal to console. And gentle, gentle as befits one who sorrows over the unrecoverable past while giving the courage to unlive it. His gift is to replace despair with repentance. It is a task of joy.

In Penance the sinner should not be commanded on threat of punishment to seek the sacrament, but warmly met and invited as by the father in Luke's tale, who is the Father of Jesus, and should be embodied in every confessor. It is a gift; it is no imposition.

The gift of Penance is the work of a lifetime. No man ever comes away from confession with all his sin removed. But every such graced exchange should plough deeper into the soil of his soul than before. One is forgiven as one grows.

The gospel implies, as I have earlier suggested, that the Lord does not sit in judgment of men, in the sense that he would make a decision who shall draw near to him and who be dismissed. In this sense, a human is even less empowered to make such a judgment over his fellow man. But Jesus did claim to be judge, in that he revealed the stance of men's hearts by provoking them to respond to him. In this sense man can, he *must* be judge for his brother. We can decree the eternity neither of ourselves nor of others, but we can ascertain with ever clearer honesty who we are and how we are growing into the full stature of graced manhood. In this way Penance is the judgment in time that prepares us for when there will be neither time nor judgment any more.

I should like to say a word in favor of penance also. It has long been the custom for the confessor to assign the recitation of certain prayers as a "penance". This is no penance at all, nor is it likely to be prayer. Ritual is where a man makes discovery of his sin, but real penance must send a man back from ritual to the substantive order of work and service. I suppose the idea of penance in this sense is of little appeal today, for it smacks of punishment, and punishment is not the fashion. People have somehow got it into their heads that the evil in their lives will evaporate at their wish. But we are born in selfishness and nurture the infection within us by years and years of action for our own convenience. The way to purge the evil of years of action is by action. I have little advice for the civil judiciary and its responsibilities towards criminals, but Dostoevsky's insight into crime and punishment may shed some common light upon both punishment and penance. As Raskolnikov is being sent to Siberia under sentence of double murder, it dawns on him, on Sonya, and on the reader that somehow the blood will not be expiated save through suffering. The suffering is not to appease an enraged nation, but to revive the heart of a murderous man. In a way the murder has been uprooted before Raskolnikov ever sets a foot towards the east. In another way, it will never finally be plucked up until he actually serves those years of imprisonment whereby he works out his freedom. Grieving for his crime, Raskolnikov confesses,

> "Did I murder the old woman? I murdered myself, not her! I crushed myself once for all, for ever...[2]

And as he sets off for his long and rigorous punishment:

> At the beginning of their happiness at some moments they were both ready to look on those seven years as though they were seven days. He did not know that the new life would not be given him for nothing, that he would have to pay dearly for it, that it would cost him great striving, great suffering.[3]

If true repentance entails true conversion, then it is much to the point for confessor and penitent to turn their concern to penance: a rigorous course of generosity to discipline heart and passions into service. Penitence without penance is little more than planning.

The Christian tradition of sin and foregiveness, then, seems to resume itself thus. We are created and nurtured by a

---

[2]*Crime and Punishment*, by Fyodor Dostoevsky, trans. Constance Garnett (Atlanta: Communication & Studies, 1968), p. 341.

[3]*Ibid.*, p. 449.

Father whose very name is Forgiveness. Our sin is that we serve ourselves, and see no one but ourselves. Through his Son and other sons, he reaches out to touch us, to strike us with guilt. The electrifying presence of our brother's purity opens our eyes to our befouled selves. Conscience comes alive; we turn our eyes upon ourselves, yet rather in repentance than fascination. We hear his call: he has but one commandment: he demands all our heart, all our strength, all our self — all for our own sakes. Our brother comes to us with the endless summoning of Jesus Christ, yet also his regardless love. We find the courage to invite him into our heart, and together we stumble upon shabby and petty scenes. It is I who am guilty. And I am light-hearted to be found out! He never commands me to submit; it is a favor he offers, and he knows it is. I am released from the very sins I discover, not simply for the admitting of them, but by finding it within me to repudiate these sins I at last allow myself to see. And since it is revealed to me that eternity is at stake, I become myself a more forgiving man. It will be my chief penance to bring forgiveness to others, whether or not they see this as cleaving to God. To forgive them I must bring them a love that surmounts what is contemptible in them, and is forceful enough to transform them beyond contempt.

To be a priest of such a ritual is to be a profoundly forgiven and forgiving man. To be penitent of such a ritual is to be a profoundly forgiven and forgiving man.

Prayer

Sir Lawrence Shipley, writing to Lord Armiton, once sniffed at an item he had found in a daily newspaper:

> "The Dean and Chapter of X have decided to discontinue, for the present, weekday morning service *in order that the cathedral clergy may devote themselves to work of national importance!*"
> (the note of exclamation is mine).

I need not remind you, who read the morning press so carefully, that this item of news was not given the honor of having a sensational black head-line at the top of the page or column. It had no headline of any degree of blackness. It was a minor ingredient of a long column of Home News, which included news of such national importance as that "Bumbledom has collected £ 37 12s. 5d. for Red Cross Flag Day," or that "Jane Shook has died at the age of 123," or that "a salmon weighing 35 pounds has been landed at Pangbourne."

What does this paragraph mean?

Or perhaps I had better ask: "What might this paragraph mean?"

1.   It might mean that someone with no sense of fitness had attempted a miserable hoax at the expense of the Dean and Chapter of X.

2.   It might mean that the Dean and Chapter of X were suffering so deeply from warshock that they had temporarily lost their reason.

3.   It might mean that the Dean and Chapter of X had not lost their reason but had lost their faith to such an extent that public prayer seemed as useless to the national welfare as an allotment at the North Pole.

4.   It might mean that the Dean and Chapter of X had lost neither their reason nor their faith, nor both, but had been compelled by their secular masters to a course of action which they meekly undertook as the price of their establishment, and as a reflex of the national conscience. Hence —

5.   It might mean that the national conscience had for all practical purposes disowned God, as of no national importance for six days out of seven; at least, in competition with Mars, who

for good or evil was now the supreme deity to receive the nation's supreme worship in sacrifice of
goods and blood offerings of human life.[2]

It might indeed mean that Sir Lawrence's nation had got
its priorities in a snarl. Alternatively, it might mean that upon
consideration the public judged the Dean and Chapter in
question to be more serviceable as air raid wardens than as
men of prayer. But he does raise a question that rises above
his particular pique: is prayer useful, for the national welfare
or for anyone's? There are some attitudes of prayer that
make easy sense: when we render God thanks for everything
we are and have, or crave his forgiveness for being faithless,
or simply speak our love to him. But when we start to *ask* for
things, to pray *for* something, several problems arise.

First of all, what business do we have asking for most of
the things we pray for? We pray for a better job, or a raise in
pay; but isn't prosperity exactly one of the things Christians
are being warned not to be clutching at? And we pray to be
rid of a headache, or cured of asthma, or even of cancer. But
will God protect us from suffering and pain when he gave up
his only Son to be crucified? And we pray when we've had
an auto accident, or when we are trying to find something
lost, or when we are about to take an examination (which
often amounts to the same thing). But isn't this forgetting
the lilies of the field and the birds of the air? All of this
praying for the good things of this life seems natural enough,
but the gospel suggests we may be beguiled by them.

So do not worry; do not say, "What are we to
eat? What are we to drink? How are we to be

---

[2]From a letter quoted in Shipley's diary, edited and published by Vincent
J. McNabb, O.P., *The Path of Prayer* (London: Burns, Oates and Washbourne,
1939), pp. 23-25.

clothed?" It is the pagans who set their hearts on
all these things. Your heavenly Father knows you
need them all. Set your hearts on his kingdom first,
and on his righteousness, and all these other things
will be given you as well. (Matthew 6, 31-33)

Prayer of petition, after all, would simply be asking God
to aid and abet our comfort and contentment — and possibly
vanity — in the world.

A second problem arises from the custom of praying for
other people. We pray for the woman who will shortly give
birth, or for Uncle Ralph who is too fond of the beer, or for
grandmother's high blood pressure. In aid of even graver
needs we solicit family and friends to pray for us. We declare
national days of prayer for this and that, and gather in groups
to lobby heaven about the war, or the mentally ill, or the
bishops. Is there really any strength in numbers before God?

The third problem is yet more crucial. What good does
it do to pray for favors at all? God is believed by Christians
to be more anxious to give than they to receive. He does not
need to be told what we need, he does not need to be
persuaded to give it, and is presumably not interested in what
we want but do not need. Is it not absurd in the first place to
suppose that creatures could ever persuade or cajole or entice
God to change his mind? And if that be so, then what could
possibly be accomplished by any sort of prayer of request?
Does it make matters any different than had we not prayed?

When I was a research student in Jerusalem, one of my
colleagues, now a professor of Old Testament in Paris, told us
a tale of his brief career in the French army as a young
artillery officer. One day while acting as forward observer he
got his coordinates somewhat skewed (by 180°), and
targeted in a salvo of howitzer fire on his own general
headquarters. Far more devastating might it be if our human
whim and will were able to call down the divine favor where
it seemed best to foolish us. Indeed, does not the entire

spectacle of prayer of petition somehow assume that God is not quite so discreet, nor yet so generous as we? It is as though God's more modest and reticent plans for the furtherance of the world's welfare might stagnate without our words to the wise. Who are we to counsel the Most High, or to presume our hearts are more extravagant than his own?

These are the problems, then, of prayer that asks for things. We tend to seek the very goods we should be detached from. We try to bargain with God by rallying more support behind us. And we humour ourselves that we can (or should) have any influence upon the divine largesse.

Writers of late have offered a resolution that goes somewhat like this. Despite the fact that our prayers can visit no change upon God's purpose, still our *own* minds can yield to change. The more a man sinks to his knees to beg the Father for help and rescue, the more vividly he comes to realize how completely dependent he is upon the Creator for life itself. Prayer plants in him an appreciation of what it means to be a creature. And when he prays for cessation of a feud in the family or relief from starvation in India or for disentanglement of confusion in our government, he gains from that prayer a streak of deeper sympathy for his brother's misfortune, he acquires a fuller sense of fellowship even with people never seen. He feels he is, after all, his brother's keeper, and is drawn to serve him all the more energetically in Christian love. And though the effect of his prayer be not in God or in India or in the persons confided to God's care, it issues in a change within himself. He is gradually transformed; he is the better man, the better believer for it.

Now this is one thought on the subject of request praying, but I must confess it seems feeble. On this view, God might as well not exist. One pretends that he listens to prayers, but beneath the postured exchange one would be listening to one's own impressive echo. It may seem to some a useful therapy, but the Christian is in a poor way psychologically if his transactions with God are staged in fantasy and pretense. A man can hardly gain from prayer a telling sense of dependence upon a God with whom he can never communicate.

The New Testament, of course, knows no embarrassment about prayer. The man with an epileptic child falls on his knees before Jesus and craves cure for the boy. Bartimaeus, the blind beggar, and the band of ten lepers, and the Lebanese woman with the addled girl-child, and the four friends who manhandled their paralytic companion and at last tore off a roof to present him — all these ask favors, and physical favors at that. The promise was there for them: "Anything you ask from the Father he will grant in my name. . .Ask and you will receive, and so your joy will be complete" (John 16, 23-24). Jesus urges his party to pray and never lose heart, like the widow who pestered the judge so often that he finally granted her relief just to be rid of the nuisance (Luke 18, 1-8). The prayer should be humble, though: more like that of the tax-gatherer than that of the Pharisee (Luke 18, 9-14).

Paul closes most of his letters with a promise of intercession, and a claim on his protégés' prayers. Timothy is told that petition should be made for public officials, that the national life may be tranquil. James sends elders to pray for the recovery of those who lie abed.

Jesus himself was one to spend whole nights in the hills, alone to pray. At the great moments in his hasty life he was said to be praying: at his baptism, during the transfiguration, at the last supper, in the garden, on the cross. For what did he ask?

> I am not praying for the world but for those you have given me, because they belong to you . . . I am not asking you to remove them from the world, but to protect them from the evil one . . . I pray not only for these, but for those

also who through their words will believe in me.
May they all be one. (John 17, 9.15.20).

What says this to our problems with prayer? First, Jesus'
prayer walks pace by pace with his work, as left foot and
right tread beside one another on one trail. Christ who cried
by the grave of Lazarus, Christ who found food for his
followers, Christ who loved the lepers and cleansed them,
cares deeply for every human need. There is no spite about
the physical, indeed no desire to spare it. But there is little
interest in these things of the body for their own sake. When
he heals a cripple or raises a widow's son from death, or
provides wine for the feast, it is all with an eye to drawing
men most personally into the Father's love. The hand holds
out more than the hand can hold. Men cannot live by bread
alone, yet through bread Jesus supplies the nurture that
provides men with eternity.

Hilaire Belloc writes:

> I am never content with the adjunction to
> treat temporal affections as unimportant. It seems
> to me false with the falsity of a half statement. It
> isn't, in itself, unimportant, compared with the
> eternal business of the soul, but it is, itself, part of
> the eternal business of the soul. The major human
> affections are immixed with eternity. That is their
> very quality. If it were not so they would not be
> major things; and when the physical side comes in,
> as with parents and child, or lovers, or husbands
> and wives, the sacramental quality appears at once;
> a thing that never appears save where the temporal
> and eternal are mixed.[3]

[3]From a letter to Mrs. Reginald Balfour, *Letters from Hilaire Belloc*, ed.
Robert Speaight (London: Hollis and Carter, 1958), pp. 225-26.

Jesus' prayer was as absorbed in temporal gift as was his work. Indeed, his prayer was a cry to the Father about what he was struggling for: to tear the heart of man from the rancid swamp of his ego, and plant him in the sweet soil of love. His prayer is as word to his gesture, the consecration formulary for the bread he holds out. He prays for those he serves, and those he reaches out to serve with other hands that lend themselves to him. It is not simply that his prayer spurs him to serve; the same Spirit that gives him force for his task gives breath to his utterances. The more the believer's prayer is absorbed into this same Spirit, the more it will leave off being simply an expression of selfish whims and cravings, and claim from the Father those gifts that give the flesh spirit. The more readily we set our mind upon the kingdom and its righteousness before all else, we shall pray for all else as a means of making that kingdom come.

As for praying in unison, the point is not to sway the Father, but to give wider utterance to a shared belief. The thrust of Christ's desire is that his address to the Father infiltrate into all human desire on earth, that the voice of men be put into counterpoint with the voice of the Son, that more and more we echo in chorus the eternal dialogue of intimacy between Father and Son. If others be asked to join in prayer, it is in awareness that the body mystical of Jesus Christ binds men in as limbs and members, quickened by a common instinct. Paul says to the Colossians:

> It makes me happy to suffer for you, as I am
> suffering now, and in my own body to do what I
> can to make up all that has still to be undergone by
> Christ for the sake of his body, the Church. (1, 24)

The suffering of Jesus was finished on the cross, but the suffering of the fuller-fleshed Christ goes on in every man that lives in faith. Paul might as well have said that his prayer was meant to complete, in his petitions, the full tale of Christ's converse with the Father. If suffering is handed down, so must prayer be.

As for trying to extort favors from a grudging God: well, that is not the point of prayer at all. It is none of our charge to rebuke God for being niggardly with his children, or to suggest that too little largesse, or ill-chosen graces have been unleashed upon our earth. There is more than enough of his favor before us. What we pray for, what we strain to work for, is that men would within themselves learn to walk upon the earth as a land graced. What one man steps over as a stone, the next will stoop to discover as a warm and fresh loaf. Our path is strewn with favor, and could be even more crowded with kindness to no effect, man being disposed to call it wilderness. As we pray "through Christ our Lord," we incarnate his desire that men discover the gifts that lie to hand, that they be fed, healed, and resurrected by the food, nursing, and fearless death we try to share with them. Our task is never to draw God's favors to the measure of our requests, but to stretch our petitions to the measure of his generosity. And this involves us in the same mystery as does gratitude: we never see clearly enough what is a benefit to thank him for, or what is a misfortune to ask relief from.

Only those who believe, pray. Only those who work, may pray. Only those who pray, work that others may believe and serve. We pray for those we serve, yet our prayer strains even to outreach our arms, to solicit for those we cannot touch. Our prayer is the muttering of men busy yet not preoccupied. Prayer does not do what we cannot; it is not our only resort when confronted with our own impotence. Prayer can bring from God only what we can do. We are in large part the answer to our own prayers, the gift for those we commend. We do not take some matters into our own hands, and leave others for the more powerful devices of the Lord. We believe that there is no more powerful achievement than to transform a man from sick and solitary selfishness to the energies of love, and this is the work put in our hands, as well as the gift of God. It is all one: we pray for what we work for, we are given what we wreak.

A distinctively Christian sense of prayer reveals that,

rather than it being an appeal to God, it is itself a reply to his call. It is not we who solicit his generosity; it is he who summons ours forth, in word and work harmonized. We are only distracted if always trying to validate prayer by its effects: in a God persuaded, in a neighbor enriched, or (by rebound) in a self made more sensitive. Prayer is itself an effect more than a cause. Rather than releasing grace, it flows from grace. Though cast into the syntax of request, prayer to the Father of Jesus is addressed to one who is supremely giving — giving even the faith wherewith we pray. Our concern for prayer should not be in what it will produce, so much as in how resonant it is with God's work in the world, and our own.

Jesus' intimates long remembered that when fallen to prayer, he forewent the ancient courtesies of their people, and addressed the Lord with startling familiarity. "Abba," he called him, in the affectionate way a boy might call his father. It made them bold to think they too might speak to the God of Abraham, Isaac, and Jacob as friendly Father. Nor was it merely a matter of titles. As they found themselves transformed by Jesus' affection, and others transformed by theirs, to their immense and ecstatic astonishment, they burrowed into the comforting secret of a common purpose and power with the Father, and addressed him with confidence, calling insistently for his favors as a son might who knows his father inside out, and is sure that his very appeals are part of a wiser and subtler scheme than he can yet know, but in which he plays his intended part. They ask the very one who bade them ask, that their joy be made complete.

So it was with Philemon. He could hardly summon himself to squander all his security for love, if he had no intimacy of conversation with the Father and Son who had taught him what cherishing might be.

And so it is for any believer, who might sit up some day

with astonishment to find that what he had gotten himself into was far more consuming than he had suspected. And so it is.

Afterword

Most authors write their preface last of all, then turn round and meet their readers with it at the threshold of their books. I would prefer to leave it last, as last written, counting on more forbearance from readers who have seen me through than from browsers wondering whether it be worth a try.

This is a book about Christian faith. The times are bewildering for faith. This is fortunate. Most of us were reared in other days when we were assured there were no sharp bewilderments. For the help of those who also grope about for some simple sights in upset days, I offer a single insight about the Father of Jesus, coherently pursued across doctrine, ethics, and worship. I offer no handbook or summary of Christian belief; this is no time to do it, and I am not capable. Nor do I infer that the point I make is at the center of Christianity, or the most important, or even the most needed for our times. All I can say is that it is integral to faith in the Father of Jesus, and when it is ignored we stray.

I touch often upon church. Most readers will be pleased

that in so doing I have not spent any time berating the bishops. Others are, I trust, as weary of that theme as I. Besides, when one recognizes these gentlemen as of such strikingly ordinary accomplishments, and so powerfully distracted from the gospel, he should rather offer encouragement than abuse. I hope not to have written another bickering book.

There are few pages here, but they are chewy. I leave them so with the expectation that my good readers will graze and ruminate at leisure, and perhaps find, as I find, undeveloped points and hints that invite further development consistent with my theme.

The book is in the Catholic tradition, as am I. But in these years when Christians from widely scattered traditions begin to make common cause and find they confront common puzzles, I expect scholars and believers in all churches will find themselves at home here. I make bold to hope even that those who have no Christian faith would find my theme inviting, as king Agrippa listened with sympathy to Paul (Acts 26, 27-29). At any rate, they will not be at a loss, like a Poor Clare reading a Freemasons' Manual.

It is a book that was nearly never written. For some years this theology had been growing within me, and finally two summers were vacated to allow for the undertaking. The very day I first set pen to paper, word came that I had been elected provost of the University of Notre Dame. The writing went on, thanks to many friends.

The Rockefeller Foundation offered six weeks of hospitality at its study center, the Villa Serbelloni, in Bellagio, Italy, at the gracious hands of John and Charlotte Marshall. Each morning I threw my shutters open upon Lake Como, and enjoyed the mountain air sent down the gorge from Switzerland. For a summer there, thanks. Also I honor the memory of Martin Gillen, a doughty lawyer who thirty years ago bequeathed to the University of Notre Dame a vast tract of lakeland astride the Michigan-Wisconsin border. Here amid his gifts of heron, pike, and deer, aspen, balsam, and birch, there is room for legs and mind alike to roam. For a summer here, thanks.

I owe appreciation also to Francis Sullivan, C.PP.S., and Ferdinand Brown, C.S.C., colleagues who staffed my desk while I crept off to write. Harry Culkin, Stephen Mysliwiec and Rita Grontkowski helped prepare the manuscript, and Charles Sheedy, C.S.C., Stanley and Ann Hauerwas, James DeVoe, Stephen Dixon, and others criticized it to its profit.

While I was a boy, we brought my great-aunt Mary to town, to lodge in a nursing home. My great-grandfather had come from Ireland a penniless donkey boy. He died a devout and faithful Catholic, but meanwhile had become a multi-millionaire, and his spoiled children one and all left aside faith in God, church, and others besides. My grandmother was the first to return to her faith, about the time that I needed to be dragged, delinquent by a year or so, to the baptismal font. When her older sister came, long widowed and anciently aristocratic, to our town, she had been many decades apart from religion, but was gently restored through the honest services of a young priest. One night we were abruptly summoned from the dinner table by a call from the nursing home, and arrived to find that great-aunt Mary, that spunky lady become mellowed, had quietly died. She had at the time been reading Augustine, and we found her *Confessions* marked at this passage in the tenth book:

> Late have I loved Thee, O Beauty so ancient and so new; late have I loved Thee! For behold Thou wert within me, and I outside; and I sought Thee outside and in my unloveliness fell upon those lovely things that Thou hast made. Thou wert with me and I was not with Thee. I was kept from Thee by those things, yet had they not been in Thee, they would not have been at all. Thou didst call and cry to me and break open my

deafness: and Thou didst send forth Thy beams
and shine upon me and chase away my blindness:
Thou didst breathe fragrance upon me, and I drew
in my breath and do now pant for Thee: I tasted
Thee, and now hunger and thirst for Thee: Thou
didst touch me, and I have burned for Thy peace.[1]

This snatch of Augustine meant much to me then, and
today it still does. It puts me in mind of Jesus' own remark at
the close of that chapter in Matthew's gospel which contains
all the riddles of his parables: "Well then, every scribe who
becomes a disciple of the kingdom of heaven is like a
householder who brings out from his storeroom things both
new and old" (Matthew 13,52). I am a scribe. My craft is the
tradition, which I must study in its antiquity and make
present for my fellows of this day. I marvel at it: primitive
yet not stale, usually loved late. This book draws, I believe,
on discoveries ever ancient, ever new: faithful to a revelation
long in coming, alert to questions never asked till now, and
resigned to the belief that all our answers are but makeshifts
in lieu of death and clearer vision.

I began with Philemon, an earnest man troubled by a
command that gave him no rest, yet offered peace. He was
offered a gospel that he could not quite master. He
responded, one trusts, to a summons that drew from him
never enough, but more and more, much more even than he
had planned to give or thought himself able to give. It
transfigured him. It put nails through him. It was worth it.
This book strains after what drew him on.

Killarney Point
Land O' Lakes, Wisconsin
Lady Day in Summer: August 15, 1971

[1]Translated by F. J. Sheed (New York: Sheed and Ward, 1943), p. 236.

The author wishes to express his gratitude to the following persons and publishers for permission to cite passages in this book:

Commonweal, for passages from "Love is the Only Measure," by Joseph Fletcher (January 14, 1966); "The Total Context," by Herbert McCabe *(Ibid.)*; "Short and Select," by J. F. Powers (August 5, 1949); and "Caesar as God," by James V. Schall (February 6, 1970).

Doubleday and Company, Inc., for passages from *The Jerusalem Bible,* ed. Alexander Jones (1966); and *The Social Construction of Reality: A Treatise in the Sociology of Knowledge,* by Peter L. Berger and Thomas Luckmann (1966).

Farrar, Straus & Giroux, Inc., for passages from *St. Francis Xavier,* by James Brodrick, S.J. (1952); and *The Towers of Trebizond,* by Rose Macaulay (1956).

Houghton, Mifflin Co., for passages from *War As I Knew It,* by George S. Patton, Jr. (1947).

International Universities Press, Inc., for a passage from *Papers on Psychoanalytic Psychology* (1964).

Journal of the American Academy of Religion, for the material in Chapter V, first published in the December, 1971 issue.

John le Carré, for a passage from *The Spy Who Came in from the Cold* (1963).